Diagnosing Identities, Wounding Bodies:

Medical Abuses and Other Human Rights Violations Against Lesbian, Gay and Transgender People in Iran

Iranian Lesbian
&
Transgender Network
(6Rang)

Justice For Iran

Diagnosing Identities, Wounding Bodies:

Medical Abuses and Other Human Rights Violations Against Lesbian, Gay and Transgender People in Iran

First Edition
Copyright. Justice for Iran (JFI) &
Iranian Lesbian and Transgender Network (6Rang) © 2014
Second Edition 2016

Published by:
Justice for Iran
www.justiceforiran.org
&
Iranian Lesbian and Transgender Network (6Rang)
www.6rang.org

Page layout: Aida Book, Germany

ISBN 978-3944191-98-0

Acknowledgments

This report is the outcome of a joint research-for-action project by Justice For Iran (JFI) and Iranian Lesbian and Transgender Network (6Rang), called "No to Forced Sex Change." The project was overseen by Shadi Amin, the founder and co-coordinator of 6Rang, who in addition, conducted fieldwork and carried out the literature review in context of Iran. The report was written by Raha Bahreini, former legal researcher at JFI. She conducted the legal research and literature review of the relevant international standards. Significant input into research was also provided by three research assistants whose names are withheld for security reasons. The report was reviewed by Shad Sadr, Executive Director of JFI and edited by Nicola McDermott and Pouneh.

JFI and 6Rang are deeply grateful to all the transgender, lesbian and gay individuals who agreed to be interviewed. The report would not have been possible without their generosity and trust.

Special thanks also to all colleagues at JFI and 6Rang who assisted with transcription and translation of testimonies, as well as research and publicity.

JFI and 6Rang also appreciate Hivos for the financial support they provided for the "No to Forced Sex Change" project

Contents

1. Introduction and Background

In 2006, Sarah, a twenty-two-year-old Iranian lesbian woman, came out to her parents as being attracted to women. While not reacting violently, her father asked that she see a psychotherapist. At his request, Sarah went through a couple of therapy sessions in Tehran that were aimed at "converting" her sexual orientation:

> The sessions did not get anywhere, leading the counselor to finally say that there is no use in continuing the therapy "because I was not willing to alter my preferences"... In our sessions together, he did not use the word "transsexual," but pressed that I have the traits and characteristics of a man. He insisted on this opinion despite my repeated attempts to refute it. He said the same thing to my dad. After that, my dad brought up the issue of sex change and to this day he continues to persist with the belief that I want to be a man.[1]

The pressure that Sarah experienced to either turn away from lesbianism or self-identify as a transsexual is not an isolated incident in Iran. Health-care professionals are apparently telling lesbian, gay and transgender people, on a routine basis, that their same-sex attraction and gender non-conformity is a sign of Gender Identity Disorder (GID) [*ekhtelal-i hoviat-i jensy*] that must be treated with "reparative" therapies or sex reassignment surgeries. Sarah was fortunate to be in a position where she was able to refute her therapist's misdiagnosis, and avoid a hazardous path that would have set her up for psychiatric, hormonal and surgical interventions inconsistent with

---

1 Interview with Sarah, 25 January, 2013.

her individuals needs and harmful to her long-term physical, psychological and emotional health.

This has not been the case for many other lesbian, gay and transgender individuals in Iran who transgress socially constructed gender expectations. Distressed with the traumas sustained due to family and community violence, and discriminated against by laws criminalizing consensual homosexual acts, prohibiting trans-dressing, and imposing sex reassignment surgery as a prerequisite for obtaining legal gender recognition, lesbian, gay and transgender people feel increasingly pressured to opt for psychiatric, hormonal and surgical treatments. This pressure is exerted through an official discourse, enforced by various laws and policies, which considers homosexuality as a form of crime, sin, and deviation, but treats transsexuality as a legitimate health problem for which the sanctioned cure is sex reassignment surgery.

The champions of this discourse, which include both state officials and state-affiliated mental health professionals, regularly distinguish between "disordered transsexuals" and "deviant homosexuals," labeling those who exhibit homosexual tendencies and gender variant expressions as belonging to one of these two categories based on whether or not they agree to undergo psychiatric and surgical treatments aimed at "curing" them of homosexuality and turning them into gender conforming men or women. Examples of such treatments include electroshock therapy, prescription of mind-altering and nausea-inducing drugs, unwanted sexual intercourse with members of the opposite sex, hormone therapy and sex reassignment surgeries resulting in sterilization, unsightly scarring, loss of sexual sensation, and a range of serious and severe health problems.

The present report illustrates the impacts of the foregoing treatments on the human rights of lesbian, gay, and transgender people, and analyzes their non-consensual nature against the background of violence and discrimination that shapes the lives of gender and sexual minorities in Iran. This includes the various ways through which lesbian, gay and transgender people are excluded from family homes, denied employment, prevented from going to school, forced to marry, sent to jails and detention centers, sentenced to flogging and execution, and subjected to "street" violence and other physical and verbal attacks in public and private settings.

The report also documents the human rights violations experienced by transgender people as a result of medical requirements imposed on them in order to obtain legal recognition of their gender. In highlighting these requirements, including psychiatric diagnosis, sterilization and genital reassignment surgery, the report underscores the plight of Iranian transgender people forced to forgo some human rights in order to enjoy others. The alternatives are stark. Obtain identification documents reflecting their gender expression and identity *or* preserve their physical and mental health by refusing to undergo sex reassignment surgeries. The former option may require transgender people to potentially harm their bodies through medical surgeries that are frequently performed in a reckless and substandard fashion, while the latter option will expose them to lack of legal recognition; arbitrary deprivations of liberty; torture and other ill-treatment; and widespread discrimination in areas such as employment, education and access to goods and services.

Coercing lesbian, gay, and transgender people into giving up their autonomy, self-determination and bodily integrity as a prerequisite for enjoying equal recognition before the law is contrary to Iran's obligations under international law to respect the right of everyone to enjoy all human rights and fundamental freedoms without discrimination, including on grounds of sexual orientation and gender identity. At the same time, failing to take steps to prevent, prohibit and redress abuses stemming from unscientific reparative therapies and negligent sex reassignment surgeries is contrary to Iran's obligation to act with due diligence to protect lesbian, gay and

transgender people against human rights violations perpetrated by state-affiliated medical professionals as well as those
working in private hospitals and clinics.[1]

Iran is a signatory to the International Covenant on Civil and
Political Rights (ICCPR), Article 7 of which provides that
"[n]o one shall be subjected to torture or to cruel, inhuman or
degrading treatment or punishment. In particular, no one shall
be subjected without his free consent to medical or scientific
experimentation." Free consent is not "mere acceptance of a
medical intervention." It is rather "a voluntary and sufficiently
informed decision, protecting the right of the patient to be
involved in medical decision-making, and assigning associated
duties and obligations to health-care providers."[2]

Iran is also a signatory to the International Covenant on Economic, Social and Cultural Rights (ICESCR), Article 12 of
which guarantees "the right of everyone to the enjoyment of
the highest attainable standard of physical and mental health."
The Committee on Economic, Social and Cultural Rights,
which monitors the implementation of the ICESCR, has
stated: "The right to health contains both freedoms and entitlements. The freedoms include the right to control one's
health and body, including sexual and reproductive freedom,
and the right to be free from interference, such as the right to
be free from torture, non-consensual medical treatment and
experimentation. By contrast, the entitlements include the
right to a system of health protection which provides equality
of opportunity for people to enjoy the highest attainable level
of health."[3]

---

1 See Human Rights Committee, General Comment No. 31: Nature of the General Legal
Obligation Imposed on States Parties to the Covenant, CCPR/C/21/Rev.1/Add.13 (26
May 2004), at para. 8; Committee Against Torture, General Comment No. 2: Implementation of Article 2 by States Parties, CAT/C/GC/2/CRP. 1/Rev.4 (23 November 2007),
at para. 17.

2 Report of the Special Rapporteur on the right of everyone to the enjoyment of the highest
attainable standard of physical and mental health, A/64/272 (10 August 2009), at para. 18.

3 Committee on Economic, Social and Cultural Rights, General Comment No. 14: The right to
the highest attainable standards of health, E/C.12/2000/4 (11 August 2000), at para8.

The circumstances in which lesbian, gay and transgender people in Iran undergo "reparative" therapies and sex reassignment surgeries barely seem to meet the standards of free and informed consent described above. The majority of lesbian, gay and transgender persons interviewed for this report recounted that their health-care providers did not provide them with accurate information about various crosscutting issues relating to sexual orientation and gender diversity. They were, for example, kept unaware that:

- Homosexuality had been removed from the second edition of the Diagnostic and Statistical Manual of Mental Disorders (DSM-II) in 1973 because it had been recognized that "homosexuality per se implies no impairment in judgment, stability, reliability, or general social or vocational capabilities."

- The World Professional Association for Transgender Health (WPATH) has affirmed that gender variance is not in and of itself pathological and that having a cross- or transgender identity does not constitute a psychiatric disorder.[1]

- International standards of care for the health of transgender, transsexual and gender-nonconforming people have recognized that not all transgender people necessarily need or want "the complete therapeutic triad [of] ... real-life experience in the desired role, hormones of the desired gender, and surgery to change the genitalia and other sex characteristics."[2]

---

1 Response of the World Professional Association for Transgender Health to the Proposed DSM 5 Criteria for Gender Incongruence (by De Cuypere, G. Knudson G. & Bockting, W. airs of the WPATH consensus building process on recommendations for revision of the DSM diagnoses of Gender Identity Disorders), May 2010, online: http://www.wpath.org/uploaded_files/140/files/WPATH%20Reaction%20to%20the%20proposed%20DSM%20-%20Final.pdf (Retrieved on 4 May 2014).

2 World Professional Association for Transgender Health, "Standards of Care for Gender Identity Disorders," Sixth Version (2001), online: →

- Numerous countries including Canada, the Netherlands, Portugal, Spain, Sweden, Germany, India and the
United Kingdom have taken steps in recent years to
abolish the requirement of sex reassignment surgeries
imposed on transgender individuals in order to obtain
legal gender recognition, but may still require individuals to undergo hormone therapy.[1]

They were also given types of medical advice that

- Pathologized homosexual orientation and gender variance;

- Assigned a diagnosis of disordered gender identity
based on social non-conformity to gender stereotypes,
including same-sex attraction;

- Gave a false or deceptive impression about the clinical
or scientific basis of psychiatric efforts intended to
change people's sexual orientation or gender identity;
and

- Misrepresented the efficacy and the potential for harm
of sex reassignment surgeries when counseling individuals distressed by their sexual orientation and gender
variance.

← www.wpath.org/Documents2/socv6.pdf, p. 3 (Retrieved on 4 May 2014). See also
World Professional Association for Transgender Health, "Standards of Care for the
Health of Transsexual, Transgender and Gender Non Conforming People," Seventh
Version (2012), online:
http://www.wpath.org/uploaded_files/140/files/Standards%20of%20Care,%20V7%20
Full%20Book.pdf (Retrieved on 4 May 2014).

1 For example, the UK Gender Recognition Act 2004 allows individuals to change their
legal gender without undergoing genital reassignment surgery. The Act also does not
require that individuals have undergone hormone therapy, but the Gender Recognition
Panel will likely expect you to have done so as evidence of your commitment to your new
legal gender identity, similar to what is described in Chapter 4.2. For more information,
see: http://www.pfc.org.uk/GRA2004.html for more details (retrieved 26 May 2014).

These practices represent serious violations of the right of lesbian, gay and transgender persons to informed consent,[1] and are attributable to the Iranian State not only because it fails to exercise due diligence to prevent, investigate and punish them but also because it enacts and enforces a range of laws and practices that severely restrict the freedom to seek, receive, and impart information on issues related to sexual orientation and gender identity, perpetuating the stigmatization and discrimination of lesbian, gay and transgender persons in health-care settings and elsewhere.

1.1. A Word on the Background

The earliest sex reassignment surgery reported in the Iranian press dates back to 1973. By the mid-1970s, at least one hospital in Tehran and one in Shiraz were reportedly carrying out sex reassignment surgeries.[2] Around this period, the Medical Association of Iran, a professional state-affiliated organization of physicians, began raising concerns about the medical ethics of sex reassignment surgeries, leading to a 1976 decision declaring sex reassignment operations ethically unacceptable except for intersex cases.[3]

This decision remained in force until 1985 when Ayatollah Khomeini issued a *fatwa* [religious edict] sanctioning sex reassignment surgeries. Ayatollah Khomeini had in fact ruled on the permissibility of sex reassignment surgeries as early as 1964 in his Arabic master treatise *Tahrir Al-Wasilah*, which he had written while living in exile in Bursa, Turkey.[4] That ruling

---

1 Report of the Special Rapporteur on the right of everyone to the enjoyment of the highest attainable standard of physical and mental health, A/64/272 (10 August 2009), at para. 18.

2 Afsaneh Najmabadi, Professing Selves: Transsexuality and Same-Sex Desire in Contemporary Iran (Duke University Press, 2014).

3 Ibid.

4 See section 2.1.4. and 2.2 for more details.

was, however, accorded little political or medical weight then as Ayatollah Khomeini was not yet a leading political figure and many of his contemporary clerics opposed sex reassignment surgeries for non-intersex individuals. This situation changed in 1985 when Ayatollah Khomeini, now the Supreme Leader of the Islamic Republic of Iran, was approached by Maryam Khatoon Molkara, a male-to-female transsexual person, and urged to issue a *fatwa* declaring sex reassignment surgery religiously acceptable.

Molkara's plea moved Ayatollah Khomeini to reissue his 1964 *fatwa* in Persian. This time, however, he conditioned the acceptability of sex reassignment surgery upon getting a doctor's prescription. Molkara underwent surgery in 1997. Over the following years, sex reassignment surgeries in Iran increased both in frequency as well as in public visibility. As of 2008, Iran was reported to perform more sex reassignment surgeries than any other country besides Thailand, leading some journalists to describe the country as "a paradise for transsexuals."[1]

What is less known about Ayatollah Khomeini's 1964 *fatwa* is the fact that it made sex reassignment surgery *vajeb* [obligatory] "when someone is in doubt about his manhood or womanhood and strongly suspects that he has the appearance of a man but is truly a woman or that she has the appearance of a woman but is truly a man."[2] According to some Shiite *hadiths* [teachings and sayings], true manhood and womanhood is inherently defined by opposite-sex attraction; a true man is one who is attracted to women and a true woman is one who is attracted to men.[3] Accordingly, when women and

---

1 Robert Tait, "Sex Change Funding undermines no gays claim" *Guardian* (26 September, 2007), online: http://www.guardian.co.uk/world/2007/sep/26/iran.gender (Retrieved on 4 May 2014).

2 Ruhullah Khomeini, "Changing of Sex, Issues 1 and 2" in *Tahrir al-wasila*, vol. 2 (Qum: Mu'assasah-I Tanzim va Nashr-I asr-I Imam Khomeini, 2000), pp. 596-598.

3 According to a hadith from Imam Reza, for example, "the rationale behind banning men from being with men and women from being with women is that such relations are   →

men experience same-sex attraction, they are thought to experience the qualities and inclinations of the opposite sex. As such, the implication of Ayatollah Khomeini's *fatwa* is that men and women are not merely *permitted* but are indeed *obliged* to resort to sex reassignment surgery if their transgender inclinations prove to be more substantial than mere whim and are accompanied by a strong interest in taking on the gender role of the opposite sex.

Interpreted as such, Ayatollah Khomeini's *fatwa* may be considered to have lent legitimacy to current policies and procedures that require transgender people who wish to obtain legal recognition of their gender to undergo sex reassignment surgery. It has also arguably affected the configuration of Iran's religious and medical official discourse on sexual orientation and gender identity which conflates transsexuality, transgenderism and homosexuality with one another, implying that same-sex desires and trans-dressing are symptomatic of a kind of Gender Identity Disorder for which the sanctioned cure is sex reassignment surgery.

1.2. How Many Sex Reassignment
Surgeries Are Performed in Iran?

Existing statistics on the number of sex reassignment surgeries carried out in Iran are inconsistent and contradictory. They are also difficult to obtain considering that sex reassignment surgeries take place in various public and private institutions

---

← against the nature of men and women as designed by God. Going against this natural and innate structure will cause the perversion of both soul and body… If men and women become homosexual, human kind will cease to exist and the world will end up in ruins," online:
http://www.isna.ir/fa/news/93012508886/%D8%AF%D9%84%D8%A7%DB%8C%D9
%84-%D8%AD%D8%B1%D8%A7%D9%85-%D8%A8%D9%88%D8%AF%D9%86-
%D9%87%D9%85-%D8%AC%D9%86%D8%B3-
%DA%AF%D8%B1%D8%A7%DB%8C%DB%8C-%D8%AF%D8%B1-
%D8%A7%D8%B3%D9%84%D8%A7%D9%85 (retrieved on 18 June, 2014).

and consist of a range of inter-related but distinct procedures.[1] In addition, a number of sex reassignment candidates
choose to seek medical care in other countries, notably in
Thailand, which further complicates the establishment of accurate statistics.[2] Some media reports estimate that the number of sex reassignment surgeries performed in Iran is around
15,000[3] while others indicate that an average of 270 sex reassignment surgeries take place in Iran every year.[4]

Doctors associated with the Legal Medicine Organization of
Iran (LMOI) tend to indicate far fewer numbers. In 2008, Dr.
Abdolrazegh Barzergar, the deputy head of LMOI, stated that
around 80 sex reassignment surgeries are carried out in Iran
every year, 90 percent of which involve cases of male-to-
female transitions.[5]

Interviews conducted with practicing surgeons give a different
yet equally inconclusive picture. They also suggest, however,
that the numbers of sex reassignment surgeries performed in
Iran are relatively high compared to other countries and re-
gions in the world. In an interview with the Guardian in 2005,
Dr. Mir-Jalali, a Tehran-based general surgeon, stated that he
had performed 320 sex reassignment operations between

---

1 These include genital reassignment procedures such as gonad removal and genital removal as well as reconstructive procedures such as orchidectomy, penectomy, genito-
vaginoplasty or labiaplasty for male to female (MtF) individuals, and hysterectomy, oophorectomy, salpingectomy, vaginectomy and genito-phalloplasty for female to male
(FtM) individuals. Moreover, not all those who apply for and receive a permit for sex
change necessarily undergo hormone therapy and surgeries. This may be due to financial
constraints, medical conditions and fear of medical complications or due to psychological
and behavioral self-identification as a transgender interested in adopting the characteristics of both genders, or living as a member of the opposite gender without actually undergoing sex change.

2 Robert Tait, "Sex Change Funding undermines no gays claim" *Guardian* (26 September,
2007), online: http://www.guardian.co.uk/world/2007/sep/26/iran.gender.

3 "Unter dem Schutlz der Mullas: Transsexuelle im Ian" *Auslandsjournal ZDF Television
Channel* (11 April 2012).

4 "270 Iranians change their sex every year. 56 percent of applicants seek to become
women" (3 December 2012), online:
http://www.khabaronline.ir/detail/260988/society/health (Retrieved on May 5, 2014).

5 "tedad-e afradi ke dar Iran taghir-I jensiat midahand [The number of Individuals who
change their sex in Iran]," *Tabnak Professional News Site* (13 October 2008), online:
http://www.tabnak.ir/pages/?cid=21203 (Retrieved on May 5, 2014).

1993 and 2005, around 250 of which involved male-to-female transitions. He admitted that in a European country, he would have carried out fewer than 40 such procedures over the same period. "The reason for the discrepancy, he said, is Iran's strict ban on homosexuality."[1] Dr. Mehrad Baghaie, another general surgeon specialized in plastic and reconstructive microsurgery, stated in an interview with Ghanoon Daily in 2013 that he had performed "over one hundred" male-to-female surgeries. [2] Dr. Soudabeh Oskouyee, a general surgeon active in the field of sex reassignment surgeries, has meanwhile stated that she performs between 30 and 40 surgeries every month.[3]

Despite persisting discrepancies, the LMOI has never issued any official statistics on the number of sex reassignment surgeries performed with its authorization. The latest figures the organization released date back to 2012 and discuss the number of applications submitted for a sex change permit. These numbers indicate that a total of 1366 applications were brought before the organization between 2006 and 2010.[4] They do not, however, show how many of these applications were approved. Nor do they explain how many actually resulted in sex reassignment surgeries. The following statistics show the number of sex change applicants between the years 2006 and 2010:

---

1 Robert Tait, "A fatwa for freedom" *The Guardian* (27 July, 2005), online: http://www.guardian.co.uk/world/2005/jul/27/gayrights.iran.

2 "gom shodan-i faryad-i bimaran-i ikhtelal-i hoviat-i jensi dar hayahooy-i jame'e [Gender Identity Disorder Patients' Cry Lost in the Chaos of Society] (18 August 2013), online: http://ghanoondaily.ir/1392/05/27/Files/PDF/13920527-221-10-10.pdf (Retrieved on 4 May 2014).

3 Dr. Oskouyee announced these numbers as part of a talk she gave at a panel organized by the Iranian Association of Sociology at the University of Tehran on 22 March 2014, online: http://www.isa.org.ir/news/6473 (Retrieved on May 5, 2014).

4 "270 Iranians change their sex every year. 56 percent of applicants seek to become women" (3 December 2012), online: http://www.khabaronline.ir/detail/260988/society/health (Retrieved on May 5, 2014).

Total number of applicants between 2006 and 2010:

Year	2006	2007	2008	2009	2010	Total
Number	170	297	294	286	319	1,366

Percentage of male-to-female applicants:

Year	2006	2007	2008	2009	2010	Total Percentage
Percentage	59.41	67.67	59.52	46.50	49.52	56.22

Percentage of female-to-male applicants:

Year	2006	2007	2008	2009	2010	Total Percentage
Percentage	40.59	32.32	40.47	53.49	50.47	43.77

The numbers above point to a definitive increase in the number of sex reassignment applications made in Iran, from 170 in 2006, to 319 in 2010. This trend is more significant when considering that the total number of sex reassignment applications brought between 2006 and 2010 was 1,366, while those brought between 2001 and 2006 numbered only 422.

In a recent study, Dr. Saberi, the head of a LMOI Commission that reviews sex reassignment applications, and a number of other mental-health practitioners opined that the underlying reason the number of sex reassignment candidates in Iran is larger than the international average is the difficulties associated with living as a homosexual and non-operative transgender person in Iran:

It is possible that there are just higher rates of Gender Identity Disorder in Iran. However, it may be also the case that patients present or are referred to psychologists more often in Iran than in other countries. In this case, the rejection of homosexual and transgender lifestyles in Iran is a key factor in making Gender Identity Disorder patients more inclined to choose one of the two dominant types of gender for themselves. This is because they cannot maintain their social and legal existence in Iran with an ambiguous gender identity. This matter [of identifying as either male or female] is of great legal importance in Islamic societies compared to other countries because these societies analyze their social issues through the lens of Islam. It is in this vein that His Excellently, Imam Khomeini, issued his *fatwa* on permissibility of sex change operations for patients afflicted with a disordered gender identity.[1]

Another demographic trend observed within the course of the past two decades is the growing number of female-to-male applicants in Iran. According to LMOI's official figures, between 2006 and 2010, 1,366 applied to undergo sex reassignment, 601 of whom were for female-to-male transitions.[2] This is a significant increase from the years between 1987 and 2001 where a total of 200 male-to-female transsexuals and 70 female-to-male transsexuals were reported to have applied for sex reassignment.[3] These numbers are very different from the

1 Mehdi Saberi, Saeedeh Sadat Mostafavi and Maryam Delavari, "Barresy-i moghayese-hyee-i ravand-i irja'-I motaghazian-i amal-i jarrahy-i jensiat beh kommission-i pezeshki-i qanuny-i Tehran ba tavajjoh deh standardhay-i beinolmelali [A comparative review of the procedures of referral of sex change candidates to the Commission of Tehran's Legal Medicine Organization in light of International Standards] (Fall 2010) 59 *Pezeshki Qanuny* 205, p. 9.

2 "270 Iranians change their sex every year. 56 percent of applicants seek to become women" (3 December 2012), online:
http://www.khabaronline.ir/detail/260988/society/health (Retrieved on May 5, 2014).

3 "Four times more boys than girls are hit by gender identity disorders" (date unknown), online: http://www.khabaronline.ir/detail/260988/society/health.

pattern observed in Western European and North American countries when the number of male-to-female transsexuals tends to be on average 5 to 8 times higher than that of female-to-male candidates.[1] According to some mental health professionals, this discrepancy is due to the dominant position of men and the profound culture of gender inequality in Iranian society.[2] Lesbians and female-to-male transgenders interviewed by Justice For Iran and 6Rang: Iranian Lesbian and Transgender Network (hereafter referred to as JFI & 6Rang) confirmed that the legal, social and cultural constraints experienced by women Iran such as compulsory hijab, restricted participation in social spheres and restricted mobility due to women's traditional role in the family, created a strong incentive for them to apply for sex change.[3] Despite this, the number of women who follow through with sex reassignment surgeries and change their legal gender does not seem to be as high as those who apply to receive permit to undergo sex change. According to the medical deputy head of LMOI, 90 percent of those who receive a favorable decision from the LMOI and undergo sex reassignment surgeries are male-to-female patients.[4] Dr. Mir-Jalili, one of the most active surgeons in the area of sex reassignment surgeries, similarly states that of the 488 patients he has operated on during his 20 years of practice, 408 were men and only 80 were women.[5]

---

1 Transgender Mental Health: Discussions of Mental Health Issues for Gender Variant and Trangender Individuals, Friends and Family with posts by NYC Psychotherapist Ami B. Kaplan, LCSW, online: http://tgmentalhealth.com/tag/prevalence/ (retrieved 18 June 2014).

2 Dr. Hamid Reza Attar and Dr. Maryam Rasoulian, "Tashkhiz-i avvalyeh-i ikhtelal-i hoviat-i jensi [The Initial Determination of Gender Identity Disorder]" (2003) 3 *Andisheh va Raftar* 10.

3 Interview with Farnaz, May 2012, Cologn, Germany.

4 "saly 80 nafar dar Iran taghir-i jensiat midahand [Every year, 80 persons undergo sex change in Iran] *Alef*, 30 September 2008, online: http://alef.ir/vdcau6ne.49neu15kk4.html?33122 (Retrieved on 4 May 2014).

5 "negahi be vazyiat-i bimaran-i dochar-i ikhtelal-i hoviat-i jensi dar Iran [a look at the situation of Gender Identity Disorder Patients in iran]" *Sociology Articles* (3 June 2007), online: http://sociology82.blogfa.com/post-83.aspx (Retrieved on May 5, 2014).

1.3. Organization of the Report

To date, Iranian laws and practices that criminalize consensual sexual conduct between members of the same sex and subject lesbian, gay, bisexual and transgender people to torture and other cruel, inhuman and degrading treatment or punishment have been the subject of numerous human rights reports.[1] The present report is, however, the first attempt to examine the interaction between these criminal laws and legal and medical practices that have the purpose or effect of coercing lesbian, gay and transgender persons into "reparative" therapies and sex reassignment surgeries.

It is also the first human rights report to collect the accounts and testimonies of lesbian, gay and transgender individuals who have been subjected to harmful "reparative" therapies and grossly negligent sex reassignment surgeries, and to analyze them through a human rights framework. The report is also unique for interviewing a relatively large and diverse group of individuals from the lesbian, gay and transgender community of Iran, including people living inside the country as well as abroad.

The rest of the report is divided into five main chapters:

Chapter 2 provides a summary of the applicable international standards, particularly in the areas of non-discrimination and equality, equal recognition before the law, prohibition of torture and other cruel, inhuman and degrading treatment, the right to the highest attainable standard of health, and freedom of information.

---

1 See e.g. Human Rights Watch, *We are a Buried Generation: Discrimination and Violence against Sexual Minorities in Iran* (15 December, 2010), online:
http://www.hrw.org/reports/2010/12/15/we-are-buried-generation-0 (Retrieved on May 5, 2014); Iran Human Rights Documentation Centre, Denied Identity: Human Rights Violations against Iran's LGBT Community (November 2013), online: http://www.iranhrdc.org/english/publications/reports/1000000398-denied-identity-human-rights-abuses-against-irans-lgbt-community.html#.U2eFj_2H4ds (Retrieved on May 5, 2014).

Chapter 3 provides an account of the religious and legal background and context to the approach of the Iranian Government to the issue of transsexuality, and the integral connection that this approach has with the Government's position on homosexuality.

Chapter 4 provides an overview of existing legal gender recognition procedures that make change in one's legal gender contingent on the fulfilment of invasive medical requirements, and illustrates their adverse impact on the human rights of transgender people through individual case studies.

Chapter 5 documents some of the human rights abuses that lesbian, gay and transgender people commonly experience in health-care settings in Iran based on their sexual orientation and gender identity. Two sets of abusive practices are focused upon in particular; namely, harmful "reparative" therapies" intended to "cure" homosexuality, and negligent sex reassignment procedures administered without free and informed consent, and in reckless or wanton disregard of international standards of care for the health of transsexual and transgender people.

Chapter 6 draws conclusions and identifies both general and sector-specific recommendations.

1.4. Methodology

The information included in this report was collected through extensive interviews with Iranian lesbian, gay, and transgender people both in Iran and abroad. Between February 2011 and November 2013, JFI & 6Rang interviewed a total of 95 people, consisting of 7 male-to-female transsexual individuals, 24 female-to-male transgender individuals, 12 women with a transgender identity, one man with a transgender identity, two homosexual transmen, one homosexual transwoman, 36 lesbian women, five gay men, one bisexual woman, 3 straight women, the mother of a female-to-male transsexual individual and a psychologist. Of these interviews, 29 were conducted in Iran, 34 in Turkey and the rest in Switzerland, Malaysia, Germany, United Arab Emirate, Iraqi Kurdistan, The Netherlands, Italy, England, France, Norway, Canada and the United States. Over 80 percent of them were conducted in person while the rest were conducted through Skype. On two instances interviews were conducted through the means of chat messengers.

All interviews were undertaken in Farsi without interpretation, and transcribed and translated into English when applicable. The quotes from the interviews reported here have been slightly edited only for the purposes of brevity and clarity. Interviewees are identified in accordance with their informed consent, sought by JFI & 6Rang researchers in each interview. In referring to interviewees the report always uses their preferred description of their gender identity and sexual orientation, and their preferred pronoun.

Information for this report was also collected through in person and online discussions held with numerous lesbian, gay and transgender individuals based in and outside Iran, including a very fruitful closed community research workshop hosted by JFI & 6Rang in Kayseri, Turkey in August 2012. Workshop participants included one post-operative female-to-male transsexual, one pre-operative female-to-male transsexual, 6 lesbian women, 1 bisexual woman and 1 heterosexual woman. All were between the ages of 19 and 32 and had recently arrived in Turkey to claim asylum. The greater number of female-to-male transgender people and lesbian women approached for the workshop stemmed from a deliberate choice on the part of JFI & 6Rang to focus on this population, as their experiences have traditionally received less attention as compared to those of gay men and male-to-female transgender people.

In the context of the research for the report, JFI & 6Rang closely reviewed the various books and articles published in Iran on the subject of sexual identity, Gender Identity Disorder, and sexual tendencies and conducts, including those written by Dr. Mohammad Mehdi Kariminia, Dr. Shahriar Kohanzadeh, Dr. Mehrdad Eftekhar, Dr. Saberi and Dr. Alireza Kahani. We also monitored blogs established by lesbian, gay and transgender individuals, and approached the authors for information when required.

JFI & 6Rang contacted several psychiatrists and medical doctors in Iran who are active in the field of sex reassignment surgery for interview, but they all rejected our request to be interviewed due to lack of interest in subjects relating to homosexuality and human rights, as well as concerns for their safety and security.

2. Sexual Orientation and Gender Identity in International Human Rights Law

2.1. The Right to Equality and Non-Discrimination

The Universal Declaration of Human Rights states that "[a]ll human beings are born free and equal in dignity and rights." The Vienna Declaration and Programme of Action provides that, "while the significance of national and regional particularities and various historical, cultural and religious backgrounds must be borne in mind, it is the duty of States, regardless of their political, economic and cultural systems, to promote and protect all human rights and fundamental freedoms."[1]

Central to ensuring equal and full respect for the rights and freedoms of human beings of diverse sexual orientations and gender identities is the recognition of sexual orientation and gender identity as among the prohibited grounds of discrimination. Non-discrimination clauses in core international human rights treaties typically require states to guarantee the rights set forth in the treaties to everyone "without distinction of any kind, such as race, colour, sex, language, religion, political or other opinion, national or social origin, property, birth or other status."[2] The specific grounds of discrimination

---

1 UN General Assembly, *Vienna Declaration and Programme of Action*, A/CONF.157/23 (12 July 1993), para. 5.

2 See, for example, Article 2, paragraph 1, of the International Covenant on Civil and Political Rights ("Each State Party to the present Covenant undertakes to respect and to ensure to all individuals within its territory and subject to its jurisdiction the rights recognized in the present Covenant, without distinction of any kind, such as race, colour, sex, language, religion, political or other opinion, national or social origin, property, birth or other status.") and Article 2, paragraph 2, of the International Covenant on Economic, Social and Cultural Rights ("The States Parties to the present Covenant undertake to guarantee that the rights enunciated in the present Covenant will be exercised without discrimination of any kind as to race, colour, sex, language, religion, political or other opinion, national or social origin, property, birth or other status.")

referred to in these treaties are not exhaustive as indicated by the phrase "other status."[1]

In 1994, the United Nations Human Rights Committee, which monitors the implementation of the International Covenant on Civil and Political Rights (ICCPR) held, in the case of *Toonen v. Australia*, that States Parties are obligated to protect individuals from discrimination on the basis of sexual orientation.[2] This decision was confirmed in the later views and concluding observations of the Human Rights Committee,[3] which have urged States Parties to "guarantee equal rights to all individuals, as established in the Covenant, regardless of sexual orientation"[4] and adopt legislation that prohibits discrimination on grounds of sexual orientation and gender identity.[5]

The decisions of the Human Rights Committee have found support in the general comments, concluding observations and views of other United Nations human rights treaty bodies.[6] In its general comment on discrimination, the United Nations Committee on Economic, Social and Cultural Rights recognized sexual orientation and gender identity as among

---

1 Report of the UN High Commissioner for Human Rights, *Discriminatory laws and practices and acts of violence against individuals based on their sexual orientation and gender identity*, A/HRC/19/41 (17 November 2011), para. 7.

2 *Toonen v. Australia*, communication No. 488/1992 (CCPR/C/50/D/488/1992).

3 See, for example, *Young v. Australia*, communication No. 941/2000 (CCPR/C/78/D/941/2000), para.10.4; *X v. Colombia*, communication no. 1361/2005 (CCPR/C/89/D/1361/2005), para. 9; and concluding observations on Mexico (CCPR/C/MEX/CO/5), para. 21, and Uzbekistan (CCPR/C/UZB/CO/3), para. 22.

4 See the Committee's concluding observations on Chile (CCPR/C/CHL/CO/5), para. 16. See also its concluding observations on San Marino (CCPR/C/SMR/CO/2), para. 7, and Austria (CCPR/C/AUT/CO/4), para. 8.

5 See for example the concluding observations of the Human Rights Committee on El Salvador (CCPR/C/SLV/CO/6), para. 3 (c); Greece (CCPR/CO /83/GRC), para. 5; Finland (CCPR/CO/82/FIN), para. 3 (a); Slovakia (CCPR/CO/78/SVK), para. 4.

6 See Committee on Economic, Social and Cultural Rights, General Comment No. 20 (E/C.12/GC/20), para. 32; Committee on the Rights of the Child, General Comment No. 13 (CRC/C/GC/13), paras. 60 and 72(g); Committee against Torture, General Comment No. 2 (CAT/C/GC/2), para. 21; and Committee on the Elimination of Discrimination against Women, General Recommendation No. 28 (CEDAW/C/GC/28), para. 18.

the prohibited grounds of discrimination.[1] In addition, the Committee has affirmed the principle of non-discrimination on grounds of sexual orientation and gender identity in its general comments on the rights to work, education, social security and the highest attainable standard of health.[2]

Similarly, in its General Recommendation No. 28, the Committee on the Elimination of Discrimination against Women has observed that "the discrimination of women based on sex and gender is inextricably linked with other factors that affect women, such as race, ethnicity, religion or belief, health, status, age, class, caste and sexual orientation and gender identity."[3] In their general comments and concluding observations, the Committee on the Rights of the Child and the Committee against Torture (CAT) have also included recommendations on countering discrimination based on sexual orientation and gender identity.[4]

Drawing on the views of foregoing human rights bodies, the United Nations High Commissioner for Human Rights has confirmed that laws prohibiting sexual activity or intimacy between persons of the same sex violate individuals' right to non-discrimination and constitute a breach of international law.[5] The Commissioner has found the same for laws that

1 Committee on Economic, Social and Cultural Rights, General Comment No. 20, Non-Discrimination in Economic, Social and Cultural Rights (art. 2, para. 2) (E/C.12/GC/20), para. 32.

2 See General Comment No. 18 (E/C.12/GC/18) (right to work), para. 12 (b) (i); No. 15 (E/C.12/2002/11) (right to water), para. 13; No. 19 (E/C.12/GC/19) (right to social security), para. 29; and No. 14 (E/C.12/2000/4) (right to the highest attainable standard of health), para. 18.

3 The Committee on the Elimination of Discrimination against Women, General Recommendation No. 28: The Core Obligations of States Parties under Article 2 of the Convention on the Elimination of All Forms of Discrimination against Women (CEDAW/C/GC/28), para18.

4 See, for example, Committee on the Rights of the Child, General Comment No. 13 (CRC/C/GC/13), paras. 60 and 72(g); and Committee against Torture, General Comment No. 2 (CAT/C/GC/2), para. 21.

5 Report of the UN High Commissioner for Human Rights, Discriminatory laws and practices and acts of violence against individuals based on their sexual orientation and gender identity, A/HRC/19/41 (17 November 2011), paras. 40-43.

provide for the arrest and detention of individuals for offences relating to sexual orientation or gender identity, including offences not directly related to sexual conduct, such as
those pertaining to discriminatory dress codes that restrict
men dressing in a manner perceived as feminine, and women
dressing in a manner perceived as masculine.[1]

Of other laws and practices that directly engage the prohibition of discrimination on grounds of sexual orientation and
gender identity are those that govern the issuance of new
identification documents for transgender persons. In most
countries, official documents issued to individuals (including
birth certificates, identification card and passports) contain a
field labeled "sex" which marks the gender of an individual as
either "male" or "female." Transgender persons often experience discrimination in areas such as employment, education,
healthcare and access to goods and services because their
identification documents do not reflect their gender identity
and expression. Enabling transgender persons to obtain
documents that are in accordance with their own sense of
gender identity (male, female or third gender) through procedures that are efficient, transparent, accessible and respectful
of human rights, is essential to ensuring that transgender persons do not suffer from discrimination.

2.2. The Right to Privacy and Recognition before
    the Law

The right to privacy is guaranteed under Article 12 of the
Universal Declaration of Human Rights and Article 17 of the
ICCPR, both of which state that no one should be subjected
to "arbitrary or unlawful interference with his privacy, family,
home or correspondence." In its General Comment No. 16,
the Human Rights Committee stated that any interference

---

1 *Ibid.*, para. 50.

with privacy, even if provided for by law, "should be in accordance with the provisions, aims and objectives of the Covenant and should be, in any event, reasonable in the particular circumstances."[1]

Since *Toonen v. Australia* in 1994, the Human Rights Committee has held that laws used to criminalize private consensual same-sex sexual relations violate the rights to privacy and non-discrimination. The Committee has rejected the argument that criminalization may be justified as "reasonable" on grounds of protection of public health or morals, noting that the use of criminal law in such circumstances is neither necessary nor proportionate.[2]

In states where homosexuality is criminalized and discriminatory strict codes prohibiting trans-dressing are enforced, lesbian, gay and transgender persons are forced to be discreet about aspects of their private life in order to protect themselves from homophobic and transphobic violence. Lesbian, gay and transgender persons who are seen to be transgressing social norms frequently experience arbitrary and unlawful interferences with their right to privacy, leading to arbitrary deprivations of liberty, threats, beatings, sexual assault, rape and murder. In the context of highly gendered societies, transgender persons whose official documents do not reflect their gender identity or gender expression are at particular risk because they must disclose their transgender identity every time they want to find employment, enroll in education, obtain housing, and enter gender-segregated spaces such as schools, beaches, mosques and sports centers.

States are in breach of Article 17 of the ICCPR whenever they make it impossible for lesbian, gay and transgender persons to make personal decisions, without arbitrary interference from

---

1 Human Rights Committee, *General Comment No. 16: Article 17 (Right to Privacy), The Right to Respect of Privacy, Family, Home and Correspondence, and Protection of Honour and Reputation,*

2 *Toonen v. Australia,* communication No. 488/1992 (CCPR/C/50/D/488/1992), paras. 8.3-8.7.

the state in areas as important and intimate as gender identity, gender expression and sexuality.

The impossibility for lesbian, gay and transgender persons to express their gender identity and sexual orientation without risking discrimination, torture and other ill-treatment also constitutes a violation of their individual right to recognition before the law, which is protected under international human rights law, including Article 16 of the ICCPR and Article 15 of the Convention on the Elimination of all Forms of Discrimination against Women.

The rights to private life and to recognition before the law may be also violated by states where procedures on legal gender recognition exist but contain mandatory criteria to be fulfilled that, in effect, exclude some groups of transgender people. Such exclusion could occur when, for example, access to gender recognition procedures is contingent on the transgender person undergoing invasive and irreversible medical treatments such as hormone therapy and surgical removal of sexual and reproductive organs.

2.3. The Right to Liberty and Security of Person

Articles 9 of the Universal Declaration and the ICCPR protect "the right to liberty and security of person" and prohibit "arbitrary arrest or detention." The Working Group on Arbitrary Detention has stated that detaining someone for offences relating to sexual orientation or gender identity, including offences not directly related to sexual conduct, such as those pertaining to physical appearance or so-called "public scandal," breaches international law. In 2002, the Working Group considered a case involving 55 men arrested at a discotheque and charged with "debauchery" and "social dissension." It concluded that the arrests were discriminatory, in violation of articles 2 and 26 of the International Covenant on Civil and Political Rights, and that the detention was arbitrary. The

Working Group has since reaffirmed its position on several occasions.

2.4. The Right to the Highest Attainable Standard of Health

Article 12 of the International Covenant on Economic, Social and Cultural Rights, (ICESCR) guarantees the right to the highest attainable standard of health. According to the Committee on Economic, Social and Cultural Rights, which monitors the implementation of the ICESCR,

> The right to health contains both freedoms and entitlements. The freedoms include the right to control one's health and body, including sexual and reproductive freedom, and the right to be free from interference, such as the right to be free from torture, non-consensual medical treatment and experimentation. By contrast, the entitlements include the right to a system of health protection, which provides equality of opportunity for people to enjoy the highest attainable level of health.[1]

States that require lesbian, gay and transgender persons to undergo unwanted medical procedures, including reparative therapies, sterilization and sex reassignment surgeries, as a prerequisite for enjoying legal recognition of their preferred gender and sexual orientation, violate the right to health. Substituting their will for that of individuals, they deny lesbian, gay and transgender persons the right to control their health and body, and to decide freely about treatments relating to their gender identity and sexual orientation, without discrimination, coercion and violence.

---

1 Committee on Economic, Social and cultural Rights, General Comment 14: the right to the highest attainable standards of health (E/C.12/2000/4), para. 8.

The right to health, like all human rights, imposes three types or levels of obligations on States Parties: the obligations to respect, protect, and fulfill.[1] The obligation to respect requires states to refrain from interfering directly or indirectly with the enjoyment of the right to health, including through enforcing sterilization, sex reassignment surgeries and other discriminatory practices relating to sexual minorities' health status and needs.[2] In addition, it obliges states to refrain from censoring, withholding or intentionally misrepresenting health-related information, including sexual education and information, as well as from preventing people's participation in health-related matters.[3]

The obligation to protect requires states to take measures that prevent third parties from interfering with the right to health of lesbian, gay and transgender people. This includes the obligation to ensure that health-care professionals caring for lesbian, gay and transgender people meet appropriate standards of education, skill and ethical codes of conduct, especially in relation to quality sex reassignment surgeries, and are faced with adequate sanctions when violating individuals' health rights.[4]

The obligation to fulfill requires states to undertake actions that create, maintain and restore the health of the population. Such obligations include fostering recognition of factors favoring positive health results; ensuring that health-care professionals are trained to recognize and respond to the specific needs of vulnerable or marginalized groups; promoting medical research and health education, as well as information campaigns, in particular with respect to HIV/AIDS, sexual and reproductive health, domestic violence and harmful traditional

---

1 *Ibid.*, para. 33.

2 *Ibid.*, para. 34.

3 *Ibid.*

4 *Ibid.*, para. 35.

practices; and supporting people in making informed choices about their health.[1]

2.5. The Right to be Free from Torture and Other Cruel, Inhuman or Degrading Treatment

Reparative therapies, when enforced or administered without the free and informed consent of the person concerned, violate the right to be free from torture and other cruel, inhuman or degrading treatment. Article 7 of the ICCPR provides that "no one shall be subjected to torture or to cruel, inhuman or degrading treatment or punishment. In particular, no one shall be subjected without his free consent to medical or scientific experimentation." Consent is valid "when provided voluntarily, meaning without coercion, undue influence or misrepresentation."[2] Coercion and undue influences include "condition of duress" and "situations in which the patient perceives there may be an unpleasant consequence associated with refusal of treatment."[3]

In 2001, the Special Rapporteur on Torture raised concerns about reports that indicated members of sexual minorities were being "subjected to forced treatment on grounds of their sexual orientation or gender identity, including electroshock therapy and other "aversion therapies," reportedly causing psychological and physical harm."[4] The Special Rapporteur noted that the World Health Organization removed homosexuality from its International Classification of Diseases-10 (ICD-10) in 1992 and denounced forced treatments intended

---

1 *Ibid.*, paras. 37-37.

2 Report of the Special Rapporteur on the right of everyone to the enjoyment of the highest attainable standard of physical and mental health, A/64/272 (19 August 2009), para. 13.

3 *Ibid.*, para. 14.

4 Report of the Special Rapporteur on the question of torture and other cruel, inhuman or degrading treatment or punishment, A/56/156 (3 July 2001), para. 24.

to cure individuals of homosexuality as cruel, inhuman or degrading.[1]

In 2013, the Special Rapporteur on Torture reiterated his concerns about "homophobic ill-treatment on the part of health-care professionals"[2] which included "a variety of forced procedures such as sterilization, state-sponsored forcible anal examinations for the prosecution of suspected homosexual activities, and invasive virginity examinations conducted by health-care providers, hormone therapy and genital-normalizing surgeries under the guise of so called "reparative therapies."[3] The Special Rapporteur on Torture stated that "these procedures are rarely medically necessary, can cause scarring, loss of sexual sensation, pain, incontinence and life-long depression and have also been criticized as being unscientific, potentially harmful and contributing to stigma."[4]

Similar concerns arise with respect to state practices that require transgender people to undergo unwanted sterilization and sex reassignment surgeries as a prerequisite for enjoying legal recognition of their preferred gender. These practices fall within the definition of cruel, inhuman or degrading treatment provided in Article 16 of the CAT, because they inflict pain and suffering upon transgender people for no therapeutic and justifiable purpose.[5] The World Professional Association for Transgender Health (WPATH) has made it clear that while some transsexual, transgender and gender non-conforming people cannot feel at ease without modifying their primary and/or secondary sex characteristics, others may find comfort with their gender identity, role and expression without sur-

---

1 *Ibid.*

2 Report of the Special Rapporteur on torture and other cruel, inhuman or degrading treatment or punishment, A/HRC/22/53 (11 February 2013), para. 76.

3 *Ibid.*

4 *Ibid.*

5 M. Nowak, "What Practices Constitute Torture?" *Human Rights Quarterly* 28(2006), p. 821, quoting from A. Boulesbaa, *The UN Convention on Torture and the Prospects for Enforcement* (Martinus Nijhoff Publishers, 1999).

gery.[1] The seventh version of the Standards of Care developed by the WPATH validates various expressions of gender that may not necessitate psychological, hormonal, or surgical treatments and points to a variety of treatment options.[2]

In addition to constituting cruel, inhuman or degrading treatment, enforced sterilization and sex reassignment surgeries may in some instances cross the threshold of ill-treatment that is tantamount to torture. Article 1 of the CAT defines torture as "any act by which severe pain or suffering, whether physical or mental, is intentionally inflicted on a person for such purposes as obtaining from him or a third person information or a confession, punishing him for an act he or a third person has committed or is suspected of having committed, or intimidating or coercing him or a third person, or for any reason based on discrimination of any kind, when such pain or suffering is inflicted by or at the instigation of or with the consent or acquiescence of a public official or other person acting in an official capacity."

The application of the criterion of severe pain or suffering is relatively straightforward, particularly in national contexts where sterilization and sex reassignment surgeries are of poor quality and performed in wanton disregard of international standards, rendering transgender persons seriously scarred, injured and disfigured.

---

1 World Professional Association for Transgender Health, "Standards of Care for the Health of Transsexual, Transgender and Gender Non Conforming People," Seventh Version (2012), online: http://www.wpath.org/uploaded_files/140/files/Standards%20of%20Care,%20V7%20 Full%20Book.pdf (Retrieved on 4 May 2014).

2 These include: Changes in gender expression and role (which may involve living part time or full time in another gender role, consistent with one's gender identity); Hormone therapy to feminize or masculinize the body; Surgery to change primary and/or secondary sex characteristics (e.g. breasts/chest, external and/or internal genitalia, facial features, body contouring); and Psychotherapy (individual, couple, family, or group) for purposes such as exploring gender identity, role, and expression; addressing the negative impact of Gender Dysphoria and stigma on mental health; alleviating internalized transphobia; enhancing social and peer support; improving body image; or promoting resilience. The Standards of Care emphasize that the choice and order of these treatments may differ from person to person. See *Ibid.* pp. 9-10.

The criteria of purpose and intent are satisfied because imposing sterilization and sex reassignment surgery as a precondition for obtaining legal gender recognition is inherently discriminatory against individuals who defy gender norms and
stereotypes, and one of the possible purposes enumerated in
the CAT is discrimination.[1] The Special Rapporteur on Torture has held that intent can be effectively implied when intrusive and irreversible non-consensual treatments are performed
on patients from marginalized and vulnerable groups, notwithstanding claims of "good intentions" by medical professionals.[2]

The criterion of state involvement warrants further analysis,
considering, notably, the large degree of convergence in the
jurisprudence of different international human rights bodies
applying the prohibition of torture and other ill-treatment under their respective treaties. To provide a brief summary of
the current jurisprudential lines, it is worth comparing the jurisprudence of the UN Human Rights Committee and the
Committee against Torture. The Human Rights Committee
does not require direct public official involvement as a defin-
ing characteristic of torture under the ICCPR; a conclusion in
line with its General Comment No. 31 which stresses that
"States Parties have to take positive measures to ensure that
private persons or entities do not inflict torture or cruel, inhuman
or degrading treatment or punishment on others within their
power."[3] By contrast, the Committee against Torture, as
guided by the definition of torture contained in Article 1 of
the CAT, has clearly maintained the understanding of the
"state official" requirement in relation to torture.[4] However,

---

1 Report of the Special Rapporteur on torture and other cruel, inhuman or degrading
treatment or punishment, A/HRC/22/53 (11 February 2013), para. 37.

2 *Ibid.*, para. 20.

3 Human Rights Committee, *Giri v. Nepalxi*, Communication No. 1863/2009
(CCPR/C/105/D/1863/2009); Human Rights Committee, General Comment No. 31:
Nature of the General Legal Obligation Imposed on States Parties to the Covenant,
CCPR/C/21/Rev.1/Add.13 (26 May 2004), para. 8.

4 Committee Against Torture, General Comment No. 2: Implementation of Article 2 by
States Parties, CAT/C/GC/2/CRP. 1/Rev.4 (23 November 2007), para. 10.

the Committee against Torture has also recognized that where "State authorities or others acting in official capacity or under colour of law, know or have reasonable grounds to believe that acts of torture or ill-treatment are being committed by non-State officials or private actors and they fail to exercise due diligence to prevent, investigate, prosecute and punish such non-State officials or private actors, the State bears responsibility and its officials should be considered as authors, complicit or otherwise responsible under the Convention for consenting to or acquiescing in such impermissible acts."

In recent years, numerous domestic courts have affirmed that enforced sterilization and sex reassignment surgeries amount to a severe and irreversible intrusion into a person's physical integrity. In 2012, the Swedish Administrative Court of Appeals ruled that a forced sterilization requirement to intrude into someone's physical integrity could not be seen as voluntary.[1] In 2011, the Constitutional Court in Germany ruled that the requirement of gender reassignment surgery violated the right to physical integrity and self-determination.[2] In 2009, the Austrian Administrative High Court also held that mandatory sex reassignment, as a condition for legal recognition of gender identity, was unlawful.[3] In 2009, the former Commissioner for Human Rights of the Council of Europe observed that, "[involuntary sterilization] requirements clearly run counter to the respect for the physical integrity of the person."[4]

The United Nations Special Rapporteur on Torture has welcomed these developments and called upon "all States to repeal any law allowing intrusive and irreversible treatments,

1 Mål nr 1968-12, Kammarrätten i Stockholm, Avdelning 03, http://du2.pentagonvillan.se/images/stories/Kammarrttens_dom_-_121219.pdf, p. 4.

2 Federal Constitutional Court, 1 BvR 3295/07. Available from www.bundesverfassungsgericht.de/entscheidungen/rs20110111_1bvr329507.html.

3 Administrative High Court, No. 2008/17/0054, judgement of 27 February 2009.

4 "Human rights and gender identity," issue paper (2009), p. 19.

including forced genital-normalizing surgery, involuntary sterilization, unethical experimentation, medical display, "reparative therapies" or "conversion therapies," when enforced or administered without the free and informed consent of the person concerned."[1] He has also called upon states to outlaw forced or coerced sterilization in all circumstances and provide special protection to individuals belonging to marginalized groups, including lesbian, gay, bisexual, transgender and intersex persons.[2]

2.6. The Right to Education

Article 13 of the ICESCR recognizes the right of everyone to education and Article 2 of it requires States to guarantee that this right is exercised without discrimination of any kind, including on grounds of sexual orientation and gender identity. The Committee on Economic, Social and Cultural Rights has stressed that State Parties should ensure that a person's sexual orientation is not a barrier to realizing Covenant rights, and that persons who are transgender or transsexual do face serious human rights violations, such as harassment in schools.[3]

The right to education is also guaranteed under Article 28 of the Convention on the Rights of Child. The Committee on the Rights of the Child has stated that all human beings below 18 must enjoy all the rights set forth in the Convention without discrimination, including with regard to sexual orientation.[4] Concerned about discrimination offending the human dignity of the child and undermining or even destroying his or her capacity to benefit from educational opportunities, the

---

1 Report of the Special Rapporteur on torture and other cruel, inhuman or degrading treatment or punishment, A/HRC/22/53 (11 February 2013), para. 88.

2 *Ibid.*

3 Committee on Economic Social and Cultural Rights, General Comment No. 20, E/C.12/GV/20 (2009), para. 32.

4 Committee on the Rights of the Child, General Comment No. 4, CRC/GC/2003/4 (2003), para. 6.

Committee has "strongly urge[d] States parties to develop and implement awareness-raising campaigns, education programmes and legislation aimed at changing prevailing attitudes, and address gender roles and stereotypes that contribute to harmful traditional practices."[1]

Article 3 of the UNESCO Convention against Discrimination in Education provides that in order to eliminate and prevent discrimination, states should "discontinue any administrative practices which involve discrimination in education" and "ensure, by legislation where necessary, that there is no discrimination in the admission of pupils to educational institutions." Article 5 of the same instrument states that "[e]ducation shall be directed to the full development of the human personality and to the strengthening of respect for human rights and fundamental freedoms [and] promote understanding, tolerance and friendship."

The Human Rights Committee, the Committee on Economic, Social and Cultural Rights and the Committee on the Rights of the Child have all expressed concern about homophobic discrimination in schools, and called for measures to counter homophobic and transphobic attitudes.[2] According to UNESCO, "it is often in the primary school playground that boys deemed by others to be too effeminate or young girls seen as tomboys endure teasing and sometimes the first blows linked to their appearance and behavior, perceived as failing to fit in with the heteronormative gender identity."[3]

---

1 *Ibid.*, para. 24.

2 See, for example the concluding observations of the Human Rights Committee on Mexico (CCPR/C/MEX/CO/5), para. 21; the concluding observations of the Committee on Economic, Social and Cultural Rights on Poland (E/C.12/POL/CO/5), paras. 12-13; and Committee on the Rights of the Child general comments No. 3 (CRC/GC/2003/3), para. 8; and No. 13 (CRC/C/GC/13), paras. 60 and 72 (g); and the Committee's concluding observations on New Zealand (CRC/C/NZL/CO/3-4), para. 25; Slovakia (CRC/C/SVK/CO/2), paras. 27-28; and Malaysia (CRC/C/MYS/CO/1), para. 31.

3 "International consultation on homophobic bullying and harassment in educational institutions," UNESCO concept note (July 2011).

Echoing these findings, the UN High Commissioner for Human Rights has noted with concern, that some education authorities and schools discriminate against young people because of their sexual orientation or gender expression, sometimes leading to their being refused admission or being expelled. According to the Human Rights Council:

> Confronting this kind of prejudice and intimidation requires concerted efforts from school and education authorities and integration of principles of non-discrimination and diversity in school curricula and discourse. The media also have a role to play by eliminating negative stereotyping of LGBT people, including in television programmes popular among young people.[1]

2.7. The Right to Freedom of Expression and Access to Information

Article 19 of the ICCPR protects the right to freedom of expression and information which "shall include freedom to seek, receive and impart information and ideas of all kinds, regardless of frontiers, either orally, in writing or in print, in the form of art, or through any other media of [one's] choice." This right includes the expression and receipt of communications of every form of idea and opinion capable of transmission to others, including "political discourse, commentary on one's own and on public affairs, canvassing, discussion of human rights, journalism, cultural and artistic expression, teaching, and religious discourse."[2] Importantly, the scope of the article embraces expression that may be regarded

---

1 Report of the UN High Commissioner for Human Rights, *Discriminatory laws and practices and acts of violence against individuals based on their sexual orientation and gender identity*, A/HRC/19/41 (17 November 2011), para. 58.

2 Human Rights Committee, General Comment No. 34: Article 19, Freedoms of opinion and expression, CCPR/C/GC/34 (12 September 2011), para. 11.

as deeply offensive, although such expression may be restricted in accordance with the conditions laid out in the third paragraph of Article 19.[1]

Article 19, Paragraph 3, provides that the exercise of freedom of expression may be subject to certain restrictions but these shall only be such as are provided by law and are necessary "for respect of the rights or reputations of others" and "for the protection of national security or of public order or of public health or morals." The Human Rights Committee has observed that "the concept of morals derives from many social, philosophical and religious traditions; consequently, limitations...for the purpose of protecting morals must be based on principles not deriving exclusively from a single tradition."[2] The Committee has underscored that any such limitations must be understood in light of the universality of human rights and the principle of non-discrimination, which is inclusive of the grounds of sexual orientation and gender identity.[3]

Article 19 on the right to freedom of expression and information, thereby, protects all individuals, including lesbian, gay, bisexual and transgender persons, to seek, receive, and impart information on issues relating to sexual orientation and gender identity. In the 2012 case of *Fedotova v. Russia*, the Human Rights Committee explicitly stated that the right to freedom of expression also protects lesbian, gay and transgender persons in "giving expression to [their] sexual identity and seeking understanding for it."[4]

In a groundbreaking report on discriminatory laws and practices and acts of violence against individuals based on their sexual orientation and gender identity, the United Nations

---

1 *Ibid.*

2 *Ibid.*, para. 32.

3 *Ibid.*

4 Human Rights Committee, *Fedotova v. Russia*, Communication No. 1932/2010 (CCPR/C/106/D/1932/2010), para. 10.7.

High Commissioner on Human Rights reaffirmed the above points, recommending states to "ensure that individuals can exercise their rights to freedom of expression, association and peaceful assembly in safety without discrimination on grounds of sexual orientation and gender identity."

Essential to the respect for the right of lesbian, gay and transgender people to control their health and body is the provision of equal access to comprehensive sexual and reproductive health information and education.[1] The right to health requires that states "refrain from censoring, withholding or intentionally misrepresenting health-related information, including sexual education and information."[2] It also involves the states' "positive obligation to ensure the effective exercise of the right to protection of health by means of non-discriminatory sexual and reproductive health education which does not perpetuate or reinforce social exclusion and the denial of human dignity."[3] With reference to sexual orientation specifically, "this positive obligation extends to ensuring that educational materials do not reinforce demeaning stereotypes and perpetuate forms of prejudice which contribute to the social exclusion, embedded discrimination and denial of human dignity often experienced by historically marginalized groups such as persons of non-heterosexual orientation."[4]

Since the removal of homosexuality from the second edition of the Diagnostic and Statistical Manual of Mental Disorders (DSM-II) in 1973, the American Psychological Association has regularly affirmed that same-sex sexual and romantic attractions, feelings, and behaviors are "normal and positive

---

1 See: Committee on Economic Social and Cultural Rights, General Comment No. 14 (E/C/12/2000/4), para. 11.

2 *Ibid.*, para. 34.

3 European Committee of Social Rights, *International Centre for the Legal Protection of Human Rights (INTERIGHTS) v. Croatia* (Complaint No. 45/2007), para. 61.

4 *Ibid.*

variations of human sexuality" and that that "homosexuality per se is not a mental disorder."[1] They have opposed portrayals of sexual minority youths and adults as mentally ill due to their sexual orientation and raised deep concerns about the ethics, efficacy, benefits, and potential for harm of treatments that seek to reduce or eliminate same-sex sexual orientation.[2]

States that have enacted laws and policies censoring discussions of homosexuality impair and deny public access to credible medical information. This cannot but contribute to the stigmatization and discrimination of lesbian, gay, bisexual and transgender persons. The United Nations Special Rapporteur on the Right to Health has stated that such laws "fuel stigma and discrimination of vulnerable minorities" and "perpetuate false and negative stereotypes concerning sexuality, alienate [persons] of different sexual orientations and prevent [them] from making fully informed decisions regarding their sexual and reproductive health."[3] They also set the stage for medical abuse, in the form of "attempts to 'cure' those who engage in same-sex conduct [which] are not only inappropriate, but have the potential to cause significant psychological distress and increase stigmatization of these vulnerable groups."[4]

---

1 American Psychological Association Resolution (APA) on Appropriate Affirmative Responses to Sexual Orientation Distress and Change Efforts (2009), online: http://www.apa.org/about/policy/sexual-orientation.aspx (Retrieved on May 3, 2014). For more information see, APA Policy Statements on Lesbian, Gay, Bisexual and Transgender Concerns (2011), online: http://www.apa.org/about/policy/booklet.pdf (Retrieved on May 3, 2014).

2 *Ibid.*

3 Report of the Special Rapporteur on the right of everyone to the enjoyment of the highest attainable standard of physical and mental health, A/66/254 (3 August 2011), para. 59.

4 Report of the Special Rapporteur on the right of everyone to the enjoyment of the highest attainable standard of physical and mental health, A/HRC/14/20 (27 April 2010), para. 23.

2.8. The Right to a Remedy for Violations of Human Rights

The right to a remedy for violations of human rights is fundamental to the very notion of human rights. The Universal Declaration of Human Rights provides in its Article 8 that everyone has the right to an effective remedy by the competent national tribunals for acts violating the fundamental rights granted him by the constitution or by law.[1] This applies equally to all civil, political, economic, social and cultural rights. Article 2 of the ICCPR obliges States Parties "to respect and to ensure to all individuals within its territory and subject to its jurisdiction the rights recognized in the present Covenant' and "to ensure that any person whose rights or freedoms as herein recognized are violated shall have an effective remedy." The Human Rights Committee had made it clear that a state fails in its duty under ICCPR if it does not investigate human rights violations, seek to bring to justice those who are responsible and provide compensation to victims.[2] In its General Comment No. 31, the Committee indicates that both the "failure to investigate" and the "failure to bring to justice perpetrators" could, in and of themselves, give rise to separate breaches of the Covenant.[3]

The ICESCR lacks a specific provision requiring States Parties to provide effective remedies. In its General Comment No. 3 however, the Committee on Economic, Social and Cultural Rights noted that "among the measures which might be considered appropriate [to achieve the full realization of the rights of the Covenant], in addition to legislation, is the provision of

---

1 See also the International Convention on the Elimination of All Forms of Racial Discrimination, art. 6, and the Basic Principles and Guidelines on the Right to a Remedy and Reparation for Victims of Gross Violations of International Human Rights Law and Serious Violations of International Humanitarian Law, A/Res/60/147 (21 March 2006).

2 *Ibid.*

3 Committee on Economic, Social and Cultural Rights, General Comment No. 31: The Nature of the General Legal Obligation Imposed on States Parties to the Covenant, CCPR/C/21/Rev.1/Add.13, 26 May 2004, paras. 15, 18.

judicial remedies with respect to rights which may, in accordance with the national legal system, be considered justiciable."[1] Since then, the Committee has consistently affirmed that appropriate means of redress, or remedies, must be available to any aggrieved individual or group,[2] and that, as a measure to ensure the implementation of the Covenant at the national level, any persons or groups who have experienced violations of their economic, social and cultural rights should have access to effective judicial or other appropriate remedies at both national and international levels.[3]

The right to an effective remedy entails that the remedy must be capable of providing adequate reparations for the violation. The Committee on Economic, Social and Cultural Rights has clearly stated that all victims of violations of economic, social and cultural rights should be entitled to adequate reparation, including restitution, compensation, satisfaction or guarantees of non-repetition.[4] The Special Rapporteur on the right of everyone to the enjoyment of the highest attainable standard of physical and mental health effectively has concurred in this finding, adding that "at all times the State must be able to

---

1 Committee on Economic, Social and Cultural Rights, General comment No. 3: The Nature of States Parties' Obligations, E/1991/23 (14 December 1990), para. 5.

2 Committee on Economic, Social and Cultural Rights, General comment No. 9: The domestic application of the Covenant, E/C.12/1998/24 (3 December 1998), para. 2.

3 Committee on Economic, Social and Cultural Rights, General comment No. 19: The right to social security, E/C.12/GC/19 (4 February 2008), para. 77; General Comment No. 18: The Right to Work, E/C.12/GC/18 (6 February 2006), para. 48; General Comment No. 15: The Right to Water, E/C.12/2002/11 (20 January 2003), para. 55; General Comment No. 14: The Right to the Highest Attainable Standard of Health, E/C.12/2000/4 (11 August 2000), para. 59; General Comment No.12: The Right to Adequate Food (12 May 1999), para. 32.

4 See also General Comment No. 16: The Equal Right of Men and Women to the Enjoyment of All Economic, Social and Cultural Rights, E/C.12/2005/4 (11 August 2005), para. 21 (availability and accessibility of appropriate remedies, such as compensation, reparation, restitution, rehabilitation, guarantees of non-repetition, declarations, public apologies, educational programmes and prevention programmes), and General Comment No. 20: Non-discrimination in economic, social and cultural rights, E/C.12/GC/20 (2 July 2009), para. 40 (discrimination).

demonstrate and justify how it is discharging its obligations."[1] Potentially affected individuals must have access to information about the measures and be able to challenge their adequacy.[2]

---

1 Report of the Special Rapporteur on the right of everyone to the enjoyment of the highest attainable standard of physical and mental health, Anand Grover, A/HRC/20/15 (10 April 2012), para. 50.

2 *Ibid.*, paras. 50-51.

3. Discriminatory Laws and Practices and Acts of Violence based on Sexual Orientation and Gender Identity in Iran

Iran is one of the 80 countries in the world that have adopted laws criminalizing private, consensual sexual conduct between members of the same sex in, in breach of its international human rights obligations. It is also one of the five countries that still make particular types of same-sex sexual relations a capital offence. Iran is, however, a unique country for criminalizing same-sex sexual relations while allowing for, and indeed promoting, sex reassignment surgeries. This anomaly has been a source of surprise and confusion for many international observers who find Iran's stance on transsexuality to be paradoxical and contradictory.

This chapter sets the context and foundation for the rest of the report by providing an analysis of the legal environment and wider context of human rights violations that make it impossible for lesbian, gay and transgender individuals in Iran to live their lives with equality and dignity. As part of this analysis, the chapter also examines the religious and legal background to Iran's permissive approach toward transsexuality in order to show its integral connection with the larger social and legal framework that criminalizes or otherwise punishes the expression of homosexual orientation and transgender identity, and impose on lesbian, gay and transgender people the unenviable choice of having to undergo non-therapeutic sterilization and other surgeries in order to obtain legal documents matching their preferred gender or become easy targets for violence and discrimination on the basis of their sexual orientation or gender identity.

3.1. Iran's Legal Framework on Sexual Orientation and Gender Identity

Iran is a highly gendered society wherein people's sex/gender determines not only the rights and responsibilities that they have under criminal and family law,[1] but also what clothes they can wear, which courses they can take in universities, where they can sit on a bus or train, how far they can travel, and even which door they can use to enter government buildings and airports.[2] State policies and practices in the areas of family, education, labor, employment and politics are all based on gender stereotypes. They attempt to control and constrain the social and cultural patterns of conduct of men and women with a view to reinforcing social prejudices and customary and religious practices, which are frequently based on the idea of superiority of men to women, and on stereotyped roles for men and women.

---

1 The Islamic Penal Code sets, for example, the age of criminal responsibility for women at 9 and for men at 15. It applies certain crimes such as *bihijabi* [wearing no veil] only to women; holds the value of a woman's blood money to be half of that for a man; make a woman's testimony in court worth half of that of a man; gives men an exclusive right to murder their wives if they witness them while having sexual relations with a man; and exempts men from the punishments that ordinarily apply to murder (i.e. *qesas* and payment of blood money) if they murder their children. In a similar vein, Iran's Civil Code gives men the exclusive right to marry two permanent wives and as many as temporary wives; obliges women to submit to the commands of their husbands and fulfill their sexual needs; and denies women the opportunity to enjoy, on an equal basis with men, their rights to marriage, divorce, equal inheritance, free choice of profession and employment, freedom of movement, transfer of citizenship and nationality, and guardianship and custody of children.

2 There is only one legal provision wherein Iranian law has recognized an exception to this presumption of gender binary and that is in Article 939 of the Civil Code, which concerns the method of calculating the inheritance of intersex individuals. The first version of the draft Islamic Penal Code, which was passed by the Parliament in 2009, included a new article that concerned the punishment of illegitimate sexual relations between *khunsa* [intersex] individuals if these relationships amounted to *zena* [adultery or sex outside marriage] or *mosaheqeh* [lesbianism]. This article was, however, removed by the request of the Guardian Council, because it was found to allow for the unlawful possibility of turning *hodud* penalties into flogging and monetary penalties. The Islamic Penal Code divides punishments into three categories: *hodud, qesas* and *taazir*. *Hodud* is for crimes that endanger the moral order of social life. Punishment of *hodud* is mandatory and is prescribed by the *Qur'an*. As such, judges do not have the discretion to change them into monetary or other penalties.

Lesbian, gay and transgender people constitute an existential threat to this binary framework because they bypass the limits of its logic and challenge the established definition of correspondence between sex, gender and sexual orientation. This perceived threat is the reason for all the laws and practices that criminalize consensual same-sex sexual acts, prohibit trans-dressing, restrict access to accurate information on issues related to sexual orientation and gender identity, and impose sex reassignment surgery as a prerequisite for obtaining legal gender recognition. These will be examined next.

3.1.1. Treatment of Homosexuality

Article 4 of Iran's Constitution provides that "[a]ll civil, penal financial, economic, administrative, cultural, military, political, and other laws and regulations must be based on Islamic criteria. This principle applies absolutely and generally to all articles of the Constitution as well as to all other laws and regulations, and the *fuqaha* [jurists] of the Guardian Council are decision-makers in this matter."[1]

In Shari'a jurisprudence, homosexual conduct constitutes not only a *kabireh* [grave] sin,[2] but also a crime requiring punishment. This intolerance is derived from the Quranic story of Lut and the passages therein that reproach the men of that tribe "for approaching men, instead of women, lustfully" and "leaving the wives that your Lord created for you behind."[3] These passages do not specifically designate sodomy or other homosexual acts as a *hodud* crime requiring capital punishment. Over the centuries however, Shari'a jurists have turned

---

1 Constitution of the Islamic Republic of Iran, 24 October 1979, online: http://www.refworld.org/docid/3ae6b56710.html (Retrieved on May 3, 2014).

2 In Islamic jurisprudence, *Kabireh* [grave] sins refer to sins for which individuals will be punished in hell unless they repent and are rescued by the mercy of God and his prophet Mohammad. Individuals guilty of Kabireh sins cannot lead prayers and their testimony is not accepted in court.

3 Qur'an 7:81.

to various oral traditions referred to as *hadith* in order to define a variety of appropriate punishments for homosexual activity ranging from lashing to execution.[1]

The Islamic Penal Code of the Islamic Republic of Iran criminalizes consensual same-sex sexual acts, with punishments ranging from flogging to death penalty. According to Article 234 of the new Islamic Penal Code, which came into effect in 2013, the receptive/passive partner in *livat* [sodomy] will be sentenced to death while the insertive/active partner will be sentenced to death if he meets the conditions of *ihsan*[2] [i.e. is married and can have vaginal intercourse with his wife whenever he wishes] and to one hundred lashes if he does not.[3] *Livat* is defined in Article 233 of the Islamic Penal Code as "penetration of a man's sex organ, up to or beyond the point of circumcision, into the anus of another man."[4] If penetration does not take place, the lesser crime of *tafkhiz* may apply, which is defined in Article 235 of the Islamic Penal Code as "placing a man's sex organ between the thighs or the buttocks of another man."[5] Individuals convicted of *tafkhiz* are sentenced to one hundred lashes.[6] The punishment on the fourth conviction shall be the death penalty.[7]

Sexual acts between two women constitute *mosaheqeh* when, as discussed in Article 238 of the Penal Code, "a woman places

1 Iran Human Rights Documentation Centre, Denied Identity: Human Rights Abuses Against Iran's LGBT Community (November 2013), pp. 6-9.

2 *Ihsan* is defined in Article 234, paragraph 2, as the status of a man who is married to a permanent and pubescent wife and who can have an intercourse with her whenever he so wishes.

3 Islamic Penal Code of the Islamic Republic of Iran (2013) – Book II, online: http://rc.majlis.ir/fa/news/show/845002 (Retrieved on May 3, 2014). The English translation of the criminal code is available at http://www.iranhrdc.org/english/human-rights-documents/iranian-codes/1000000455-english-translation-of-books-1-and-2-of-the-new-islamic-penal-code.html#.U2Ztjv2H4ds (Retrieved on May 3, 2014).

4 *Ibid.*

5 *Ibid.*

6 *Ibid.*, Article 236. If the active party is a non-Muslim and the passive party is a Muslim, the punishment for the active party shall be the death penalty.

7 *Ibid.*, Article 136.

her sex organ on another woman's sex organ."[1] Article 239 of the Islamic Penal Code provides that *mosaheqeh* is punishable by one hundred lashes.[2] As with *tafkhiz*, conviction for the fourth time is punishable by the death penalty.[3]

Article 237 of the Penal Code also criminalizes "homosexual acts of a male [or female] person, in cases other than *livat*, *tafkhiz* and *mosaheqeh*, such as intimate kissing and touching as a result of lust, with punishment ranging from 31 to 74 lashes.[4]

It is worth emphasizing that Iran's Islamic Penal Code does not criminalize homosexuality per se. In other words, same-sex attractions, desires and identities are not in and of themselves illegal. What the Penal Code does criminalize however, are certain consensual sexual activities between members of the same sex. As will be later explained in this chapter, this conceptualization has opened the possibility for criminalizing homosexual activities while treating homosexual desires and attractions as symptoms of Gender Identity Disorder treatable with psychiatric and surgical interventions.

3.1.2. Treatment of Trans-Dressing

The prohibition of homosexual conduct originates from the conceptions of Shari'a jurists about God's prescriptions for the roles of men and women in a moral social order that is believed to be by nature gendered.[5] Within this heteronormative belief system, all humans are inherently male or female and each of these two types of sexed/gendered humans are

---

1 Ibid.

2 Ibid.

3 *Ibid.*, Article 136.

4 *Ibid.*

5 Paula Sanders, "Gendering the Ungendered Body: Hermaphrodites in Medieval Islamic Law," in *Women in Middle Eastern History*, eds. Beth Baron and Nikki R. Keddi (New Haven and London: Yale University Press, 1991), 74-95.

teleologically driven, fulfilling different but complementary
moral duties and destinies.[1] This is the reason for all the codes
in the Iranian legal system that discriminate between women
and men in the areas of marriage, divorce, custody, inheritance, labour, politics, and criminal justice,[2] and require men
and women to avoid contact in public spaces such as
mosques, schools, beaches, leisure centers and transportation
facilities, in order to avoid situations that are likely to cause
sin. Under this binary regime, men and women must at all
times know their "true gender" because only then can they
observe their gendered duties and avoid committing sin.
Trans-dressing constitutes a strictly forbidden behavior within
this system because it disrupts the gendered order of social
life and leads to gender mixing and, therefore, moral deprav-
ity.

There is no specific legislation in Iran criminalizing trans-
dressing. However, lesbian, transgender and female-to-male
individuals who wish to wear clothes mostly associated with
men face persecution based on laws pertaining to mandatory
hijab [veiling]. Article 638 of the Islamic Penal Code provides
that "women who appear without Islamic hijab in public will
be sentenced to imprisonment between 10 days and two
months or payment of 50, 000 to 500,000 Rials."[3] The same

---

1 Raha Bahreini, "From Perversion to Pathology: Discourses and Practices of Gender
Policing in the Islamic Republic of Iran" (2008) 5(1) *Muslim World Journal of Human Rights*
Art. 2.

2 Women, for example, attain the age of criminal responsibility at age 9 and men at age
15. Past this age, women are required to cover their bodies and hair in the presence of
adult men outside of their immediate family. Women do not enjoy equal rights in laws
relating to marriage, divorce, child custody and inheritance. Their life is worth half of that
of men under criminal laws. The position of the head of the family belongs exclusively to
men, and women must obey all the commands of their husbands and fulfill their sexual
needs. In return, men are obliged to provide their wives with maintenance. Women must
obtain the permission of their husbands before working in certain professions or trades
and they are barred from becoming judges, presidents and religious jurists. These examples
go to show why it is incumbent upon Muslim men and women to know their "true gender" because only then they can observe their gendered duties and avoid committing sin.

3 Islamic Penal Code of the Islamic Republic of Iran – Book V, online:
http://www.iranhrdc.org/english/human-rights-documents/iranian-codes/1000000351-
islamic-penal-code-of-the-islamic-republic-of-iran-book-five.html#.U2W4GK1dVLw
(Retrieved on May 3, 2014).

article authorizes judges to sentence whomever violates Shari'a laws to 74 lashes. This law applies to all women regardless of their personal religious beliefs, including to Christian, Jewish, Zoroastrian, Baha'i and Atheist women, none of whose belief systems require the *hijab*. As such, it constitutes a zero tolerance policy toward any lesbian, transgender or female-to-male person who may, for example, wish to cut her hair short, stop wearing the *hijab*, wear androgynous or gender-neutral clothing or express the so-called "masculine" side of her identity.

Similar restrictions are faced by gay, transgender and MtF persons who wish to express their gender identity through make-up, dress and mannerisms that are typically regarded as "feminine." Article 101 of the Islamic Penal Code (*Ta'zirat*) authorizes judges to sentence to 74 lashes those who engage in a conduct that is "*haram*" [religiously forbidden] or "offends public morals."[1] Trans-dressing constitutes a *haram* conduct within the meaning of this provision as most Shari'a jurists posit that wearing the clothes of the opposite sex on a regular basis violates Shari'a unless one does so within the confines of one's house or on a temporary or exceptional basis.[2]

3.1.3. Treatment of Transsexuality

Shari'a jurists have always recognized that there are intersex individuals, known otherwise as *khunsa*, who are neither male nor female, and who as such present a serious dilemma in a society where so impenetrable a boundary is drawn between men and women. In order to deal with this challenge, Shari'a

---

1 Islamic Penal Code of the Islamic Republic of Iran – Books I-II, online: http://www.iranhrdc.org/english/human-rights-documents/iranian-codes/1000000455-english-translation-of-books-1-and-2-of-the-new-islamic-penal-code.html#.U2W3cq1dVLw (Retrieved on May 3, 2014).

2 Shadi Sadr, Majmooyeh-I Qvanin-i va Mogharrarat-i Poushesh dar Jomhouri-I Islami [The Collection of Dress Codes and Regulations in the Islamic Republic of Iran] (Nili Book: Tehran, 2009), pp. 188-190.

jurists have traditionally outlined various criteria for assigning a gender role to intersex persons. More recently, with the advent of modern science, they have advocated the removal of sexual ambiguity through surgical remedies. In this context, physical alteration to the body has been understood not as an act of interference in God's creation but as an attempt to uncover the truth about an individual's hidden sex.[1]

Until the *fatwa* of Ayatollah Khomeini in 1964-5 though, this approach toward sex assignment surgeries applied only to intersex individuals. Shari'a jurists generally distinguished between *khunsa physici* [physically intersex] and *khunsa ravani* [psychologically intersex] and held that members of the latter group, who do not present any ambiguity in their sex organs, must not undergo sex reassignment surgeries.[2] "If they have resorted to this non-lawful action," Ayatollah Seyyed Yusef Madani Tabrizi, for example, wrote, "they have sinned; as to religious duties, they are bound by those incumbent prior to the change in their appearance."[3]

In his infamous *fatwa* issued in 1986, Ayatollah Khomeini broke away from this tradition and determined the permissibility of sex reassignment surgeries for transsexual people. This *fatwa* was grounded in a lengthier *fatwa* that Ayatollah Khomeini had first issued in his book *Tahrir Al-Wasilah*, which was written in 1964-65 when Ayatollah Khomeini was still in exile in Bursa, Turkey. Informed by the earlier rulings of Islamist jurists on intersex conditions,[4] this *fatwa* analyzed

---

1 Elizabeth M. Bucar, "Bodies at the Margins: The Case of Transsexuality in Catholic and Shia Ethics" (2010) 38(4) *Journal of Religious Ethics* 601; Paula Sanders, "Gendering the Ungendered Body: Hermaphrodites in Medieval Islamic Law" in *Women in Middle Eastern History*, eds. Beth Baron and Nikki R. Keddi (New Haven and London: Yale University Press, 1991).

2 Seyed Hossein Hashemi, "Fazlollah va taghire jensiat az manzare Quran" [Allah and Sex Change from the Perspective of Quran" (2011) 65-66 *Quranic Studies*155.

3 Ziba Mir-Hosseini, *Islam and Gender: The Religious Debate in Contemporary Iran* (Princeton, N.J.: Princeton University Press, 1999), pp. 35-37.

4 Afsaneh Najmabadi, "Transing and Tanspasing Across Sex-Gender Walls in Iran" (2008) 36(3-4) Women's Studies Quarterly 23-42, online: http://dash.harvard.edu/bitstream/handle/1/2450776/Najmabadi_Transing.pdf   (Re-

the permissibility of sex reassignment surgeries in a section entitled "The Examination of Contemporary Questions." Written in the response style of question and answer typical of Shari'a epistles, the *fatwa* read:

> The prima facie [*al-zahir*] view is against prohibiting the changing, by operation, of a man's sex to that of a woman or vice versa; likewise, the operation [in the case] of an intersex is not prohibited in order that he or she may become incorporated into one of the two sexes. Does sex change become obligatory upon a man if he perceives, in himself, the desires and inclinations of a woman or some qualities of femininity, or [similarly] upon a woman, if she perceives, in herself, the desires and inclinations which are among the type of inclinations of a man or some qualities of masculinity? The prima facie view is that it [sex change] is not obligatory; but that is the case when the person is truly a man or a woman and he or she merely notices the inclinations or some of the qualities of the opposite sex in him or herself, and wishes, now that sex change has become possible, to change to the opposite sex, [and] not when someone is in doubt about his manhood or womanhood and strongly suspects that he has the appearance of a man but is truly a woman or that she has the appearance of a woman but is truly a man. In the latter case, it is obligatory to undergo surgery, changing the superficial sex to the true sex.[1]

In this analysis, transsexual persons, known previously in the jurisprudence as *khunsa ravani* [psychologically intersex] were effectively placed in the same position as *khunsa physici* [physi-

---

trieved on May 3, 2014); Afsaneh Najmabadi, "Mapping Transformations of Sex, gender and Sexuality in modern Iran" (2005) 49(2) *Social Analysis* 72.

1 Ruhullah Khomeini, "Changing of Sex, Issues 1 and 2" in *Tahrir al-wasila*, vol. 2 (Qum: Mu'assasah-I Tanzim va Nashr-I asr-I Imam Khomeini, 2000), pp. 596-598 [emphasis added].

cally intersex], and allowed to undergo sex reassignment surgery in order to ensure their sex and gender match. This aspect of Ayatollah Khomeini's *fatwa*, which has placed transsexual and intersex persons in proximity of one another, has been extensively celebrated for paving the way for sex reassignment surgeries in Iran, and leading the government to stop lumping transsexual and transgender persons into the category of *hamjensbaz* [a derogatory term used in Persian for homosexuals] and subject them to arbitrary deprivations of liberty, torture and other forms of ill-treatment.

Critical attention is yet to be paid, however, to the manner in which Ayatollah Khomeini's *fatwa* ties the categories of homosexual and transsexual to one another. According to Ayatollah Khomeini's *fatwa*, sex reassignment surgeries go beyond being merely *jayez* [permissible] and become *vajeb* [obligatory] when "someone is in doubt about his manhood or womanhood and strongly suspects that he has the appearance of a man but is truly a woman or that she has the appearance of a woman but is truly a man."

While not outlined explicitly, the criteria for labeling an individual as truly a man or a woman includes, by necessity, a specifier pertaining to heterosexual attraction. A "true man" is one who is inclined toward women and a "true woman" is one who is inclined to men as any other than this would be tantamount to committing a grave sin. The implication of this presumption is that a woman must have a masculine soul if she is persistently attracted to women, and a man must have a feminine soul if he is persistently attracted to men. This is particularly so if the sexual orientation of such men and women is accompanied by a marked aversion to the normative mannerisms of the gender they have been assigned at birth. In these situations, Ayatollah Khomeini declares that his followers must undergo sex reassignment surgeries in order to successfully uncover the truth about their sex and make it agree with their "true gender." For Ayatollah Khomeini, this is a *mandatory obligation* because heteronormative coherence between one's sex, gender and sexual orientation is absolutely essential for the observance of one's moral and public duties as a Muslim living in a gendered society.

The *fatwa* of Ayatollah Khomeini on sex reassignment surgeries has proved controversial among both Shi'a and Sunni jurists. Many continue to see sex reassignment surgery as a mutilation of healthy bodies and interference in God's creation. Some like Allameh Mohammad Fazlallah go as far as viewing sex reassignment surgery "as nothing but a deceitful act that the Western homosexual minority undertakes in order to promote *livat* [sodomy]."[1] Nevertheless, owing to his political and religious stature, Ayatollah Khomeini's *fatwa* has been able to change the views of some Shi'a jurists and configure the discourse through which Iranian authorities currently understand and discuss issues relating to homosexuality and transsexuality.

3.1.4. Restrictions on the Right to Freedom of Expression and Information

Iran operates a vast censorship apparatus that actively censors, withholds or intentionally misrepresents health-related information on issues related to sexual orientation and gender identity.

Article 15(B) of the Cyber Crime Act sets out a penalty of 91 days to one year of imprisonment and a fine between 5 million and 20 million Rials for anyone who uses online and digital communications – including social media, blogs, and websites – to incite the public to "participate in crimes against chastity ... or acts of sexual perversion."[2] The Cyber Crime Act tasks a "Committee Charged with Determining Offensive

---

1 Ibid., at156.

2 The full text of the Act can be found on the official website of the Iranian Cyber Police, online: http://www.cyberpolice.ir/page/2431 (Retrieved on May 3, 2014).

Content" with identifying and blocking sites that carry prohibited content, and with communicating the standards to be used for identification of unauthorized websites to the Telecommunications Company of Iran, the Ministry of Information and Communication Technology and major Internet Service Providers. To date, this Committee has provided a list of 78 topics of forbidden content, including "stimulation, encouragement, persuasion, threats or invitation to immoral acts, prostitution, crimes against chastity or sexual perversion" as well as redistribution and re-publication of any content that "violates public decency."[1]

Similar restrictions are applied to the print media in order to suppress and censor discussion of issues related to homosexuality. Article 6(2) of the Press Law imposes a prohibition upon "promotion of prostitution and vice, and publication of photos, images and articles found to be against public decency."[2] Circular Number 660 of the Supreme Council for Cultural Revolution meanwhile bans publications from crossing boundaries that may result in anti-family propaganda, the weakening of family values and the "promotion of deviant and immoral individuals and movements."[3]

Provisions criminalizing the dissemination and diffusion of any positive information about homosexuality have deprived members of the public including students and health-care professionals of the opportunity to access essential information and education on issues related to sexual orientation and gender identities. Zahra Noyee, a behavioral psychologist trained

---

1 The full text of The List of Examples of Criminal Content can be found on the official website of Iran's Cyber Police, online: http://www.cyberpolice.ir/page/2551 (Retrieved on May 3, 2014).

2 The full text of the Press Law can be found on the official website of the Ministry of Culture and Islamic Guidance, online: http://press.farhang.gov.ir/fa/rules/laws2 (Retrieved on May 3, 2014).

3 Circular Number 660 Article 3, Section C (6). The text of this circular is available on the official website of the Iranian Supreme Council for Cultural Revolution, online: http://www.iranculture.org/fa/simpleView.aspx?provID=1722 (Retrieved on May 3, 2014).

at the Tehran Psychiatric Institute of Iran University of Medical Sciences told JFI & 6Rang the following about the type and quality of information and education provided to students of psychology:

> I did my studies at the Tehran Psychiatric Institute of Iran University of Medical Science, which is a very good school in this field, and yet we never learned anything about homosexuality. We just learned that if a patient is distressed with his/her sexuality, then he/she must be suffering from a disorder. We never learned anything about homosexuals comfortable with their sexual orientation. This issue was completely excluded from our course syllabuses and we were kept in the dark about it.

Professors who contravene codes of censorship and silence and discuss homosexuality in class can face serious reprisals.[1] As it will be illustrated in the rest of the report, this knowledge deficit has contributed to perpetuating stigma at and discrimination against lesbian, gay and transgender persons, placing them at an increased risk of human rights violations from both state and non-state actors.

3.2. Violence and Discrimination against Lesbian, Gay and Transgender People

3.2.1. Arbitrary Arrests and Detention and Police Abuse

Human rights violations against lesbian, gay and transgender people in Iran have their foundation in the legal framework

---

1 A recent example is the reported dismissal of a sociology professor from Allameh Tabbatabii University on the basis of an allegation that she discussed homosexuality in her class. See Hossein Alizadeh, "Sociology Professor Fired in Iran for Discussing Homosexuality?" Huffington Post, 16 September 20130, online:
http://www.huffingtonpost.com/hossein-alizadeh/sociology-professor-fired-in-iran-for-discussing-homosexuality_b_3916652.html (Retrieved on May 3, 2014).

that prohibits, with penalties including imprisonment or even death, same-sex consensual sexual conduct and the perceived expression of gay, lesbian and transgender identities. The police and the paramilitary *basij* militia routinely arrest, detain and abuse lesbian, gay and transgender individuals not based on their sexual behavior but rather based on the perception of their sexual orientation, as derived from their dress or demeanor. This is particularly true for lesbian women and female-to-male transgender persons who defy mandatory veiling and other restrictive dress codes imposed on women.

Throughout the research for this report, JFI & 6Rang received numerous reports of arbitrary arrests and detention of people solely because of their real or perceived sexual orientation or gender identity. Mahyar is a female-to-male transgender who was arrested by the police in 2001 after they asked for his driving license and realized that he is not wearing a headscarf even though he is biologically a female. He told JFI & 6Rang:

> I had borrowed the motorcycle of my brother's friend to ride around Tehran. Back then I had not received any hormone therapy and did not have a beard yet. So I looked underage and the police officer who stopped me must have thought that I did not hold a driver's license. He ordered me to pull over to the side and asked how old I am. He did not believe it when I said I was seventeen years old and said I looked like a thirteen or fourteen year old...Then he tried to body search me to see if I had any weapons on me...When he touched my body, he felt my breasts, and asked: "what are these bumps? Are you a girl?" When I nodded my head, he began yelling "what are you doing here then, in the streets, without a uniform and headscarf?"

> He asked the officer standing next to him to bring me a headscarf to cover my hair. He was handed a

scarf from inside the police car and asked me to put it over my head. They then pushed me inside the car and began beating me severely. They hit me so much in my face and head that I started feeling numb. Only now and then I could feel the blows from the left and right... They said that I must be psychologically tested because a mentally sane woman, who knows about the country's laws, would never come out to the streets without a headscarf. I was then arrested and taken to a police detention center. I was released the next day after I signed a letter of repentance.[1]

Akan's Story

Akan is another female to male transgender person who was arrested and ill-treated because of not wearing a headscarf:

"I cannot even tell you how many times I have been harassed and assaulted by the police and the Basij because of my dress. One time in December 2009, I was walking with my girlfriend in the streets Mahmoud Abad, Mazandan in northern Iran late at night. A few *Basijis* stopped us because they thought we are girlfriend and boyfriend. They asked for our identification cards. I panicked and told them that I am actually a girl and I came out like this [wearing what is considered "masculine" clothing] because I wanted to buy a telephone card to call my mother who lives in a different town for something urgent and I did not feel safe to leave the house at this time of the night dressed as a woman.

Their eyes glared and they looked at me as if they had caught a dangerous criminal. They pushed me into their car. There were three of them. The one who had asked for my identification card would not take his eyes off me and repeatedly asked

---

1 Interview with Mayhar, July 2012.

if I was really a girl. He would laugh at me and touch my body. I would ask him to get his hands off my body and that who I am was none of his business. The man who was sitting in the front row shouted that I have no right to speak to them this way and I should just shut my mouth up. I was really scared because they did not stop touching my. They put their hands on my breasts and between my legs. They said they wanted to know if I was really a girl or boy. I don't know if they had never encountered someone like me or if that was just their way of harassing me.

They took me to a police detention centre and kept me there for the night with two other girls who had been arrested for bad-hijabi [failing to wear the veil properly]. I was released the next day after signing a letter of repentance, promising that I will never dress like that in public again. I was told that I should be grateful that I was not charged and taken to the court."[1]

A few of the transgender individuals interviewed for the report noted that they were able to avoid arrest and detention when they provided the police with documents proving that they were undergoing sex reassignment procedures. Hasti, a self-described male-to-female transsexual, for example, told JFI & 6Rang that, "the police has in recent years let us go free when they find out that we are transsexuals. I am not sure if this is due to the military exemptions issued to transsexuals, which has enhanced the knowledge of the police about us or of it is because the Legal Medicine Organization allows sex change in Iran." Nevertheless, police abuse remains a widespread and common reality for many lesbian, gay and transgender people.

---

1 Interview with Akan, February 2011.

Kaveh's Story

Kaveh is a female-to-male transgender person. He described to JFI & 6Rang that he was verbally and sexually harassed after he informed a police officer that his legal sex was female:

"I told the police officer that I used to be a girl before but I am now a boy and showed him my sex reassignment certificate. I did not give him my old driving license, even though I had it with me, because I knew that seeing that would make him ridicule me even more. I told him I have surrendered my old driving license and can't get a new one until I am issued a new identification document reflecting my gender. He was puzzled and asked if that meant I had already had my surgery. I used to flatten my breasts by strapping them tightly against my body, so even if some one touched them, they would not be able to notice them. He touched my chest and said to his colleagues, "she's telling the truth. She has not got anything." He then asked: "So what have you got down there now?" He was standing very close to me, almost whispering to me. I said, "I have [a penis.]" He said he would like to touch it but I pulled back and said that I do not appreciate that. He really meant to touch me; this is how audacious they are. He said: "Come on! You're a boy now! Boys are not shy about these matters with each other. Forget your past girly habits!"… I resisted but he continued insisting.

The situation at that point was quite intimidating: The four of them had surrounded me, and I was young, short and extremely agitated. Thank God that at that very moment my two friends, whom I was waiting for, arrived. They were both girls. He asked who they were. I said they were my friends from high school, and we were meeting to catch up. I was lucky they did not question my friends. He said: "You enjoy being surrounded by all these girls, ha?" I found the way he spoke very offensive but I tried to remain calm and to chill out with them so that they would let me go, and they finally did."[1]

Almost every lesbian, gay and transgender interviewee who did not conform to culturally approved models of femininity and masculinity told JFI & 6R that they lived in fear of being sexually assaulted and raped by members of the police and *Basij*. For several of them, this fear had unfortunately come true.

Shiva's Story

Shiva, a male-to-female transgender, described to JFI & 6Rang how she was sexually abused by three police officers in 2009:

I often got into trouble with the authorities because of the way I dressed and styled my hair. They would stop me because of it and begin asking questions. Once, I made the police very angry because I returned their insults with insults and so instead of taking me to the police station, they took me the basement of this mosque that was next to their station in Narmak neighborhood in Tehran. There, three police officers raped me, and burned my skin with cigarettes.

One could have lost his life under their beatings and torture. I begged them to kill me but they did not. I was twenty-eight years old back then and they were around the same age. They were quite a sick team. They told me that they filmed the sexual incident and they would distribute it to blackmail me… I never allowed my family to find out about the incident… Seeing the cigarette burn scars on my body still distresses me and I always have to cover my body whenever I go out.[2]

---

1 Interview with Kaveh, January 2013.

2 Interview with Shiva September 2013.

Raids on Private Parties

In Iran, laws designed to forbid people from freely expressing their sexual orientation and gender identities become a foundation for the control of people's behavior not only in public but also in private spaces. Most egregiously, they provide an excuse for the police and other state actors to raid private gatherings that neighbors or other informants report to be attended by "homosexuals," and to arrest the attendees in the absence of any evidence that a crime has been committed, and simply on the basis of their dress or demeanor.

Since 2007, there have been several confirmed reports of state-led raids on private parties followed by mass arrest and detention of those suspected of "homosexuality."[1] Detainees are reported to have been beaten, and subjected to other cruel, inhuman or degrading treatments or punishments, including anal examinations by medical doctors without consent.[2] In many cases, intelligence forces are believed to have carried out the raids while in at least one case in the western city of Kermanshah, the intelligence unit of the Revolutionary Guards took responsibility for the raid.[3]

The Kermanshah Raid, 8 October 2013

On Thursday 10 October 2013, the news website of the Revolutionary Guards in Kermanshah province, reported that their forces had dismantled what it claimed to be "a network

---

1 Human Rights Watch, "Iran: Private Homes Raided for 'Immorality'" (28 March 2008), online: http://www.hrw.org/en/news/2008/03/27/iran-private-homes-raided-immorality (Retrieved 18 June 2014).

2 See, for example. Amnesty International, "Joint Open Letter to Iranian President Rouhani" MDE 13/058/2013 (20 December 2013), online:

http://www.amnesty.org/en/library/asset/MDE13/058/2013/en/f28e3e81-f329-48fc-8c7c-e23ea88dc750/mde130582013en.html (Retrieved 18 June 2014).

3 Iranian Lesbian & Transgender Network "Mass Arresr in Kermanshah on Charges of Homosexuality" (14 October 2013), online: http://6rang.org/fa/news/a-group-of-gay-men-have-been-arrested-in-kermanshah /(Retrieved 18 June 2014).

of dozens of *Hamjensbaz* and Satanists." The website added that the network "was dismantled after several months of monitoring and surveillance by the Revolutionary Guards security forces."

The raid took place on Tuesday night when some 80 people had gathered for a birthday party in Kermanshah. The forces reportedly started beating everyone, while swearing that "You're not men, you're a bunch of women. You've gathered here to rape each other. The government will never accept you. Faggot asses! [Korreh-khar'ha'ye Hamjensbaz]."At least 17 people who had tattoos, make-up, or were wearing rainbow bracelets were arrested and taken to an unknown location while blindfolded. At the detention center, they were reportedly stripped of their clothes, and photographed naked. They were interrogated about the details of their sexual relationships and repeatedly beaten to "confess" to being "homosexual and Satan worshippers." The detainees were eventually released by October 14 after posting large bails. Their court dates, which were originally scheduled for October 11, were cancelled.

The Esfahan Raid, 10 May 2007

In May 2007, during a nationwide crackdown on modes of dress and conduct deemed to be "un-Islamic," the police raided a private party in an apartment building in the central city of Esfahan and arrested 87 persons, including four women and at least eight people whom they accused of crossdressing. Ali, one of the 87 men arrested, told JFI & 6Rang about the abuses that the detainees experienced at the time of their arrest and during their four week detention:

"It was twenty or thirty minutes into the party when I heard the sound of something breaking. The music was loud and the guests were either dancing or taking pictures. I was asking someone if a fight was going on when all of the sudden, doz-

ens of police officers wearing camouflage uniforms and holding batons, poured into the party room and ordered everybody to lie down on the floor. Everybody was scared and
screaming. We lay prostrate on the floor and clasped our
hands behind our heads. Convulsed with fear, some guests
were vomiting foam. They started beating us harshly and
walked over us with their boots.

They handcuffed me, pulled my t-shirt over my head, and
took me down two sets of stairs while still beating and kicking
me. I was put, along with twenty to thirty other people, in a
van and taken to the detention center. As soon as we got off
the van, they started beating and kicking us to the point that
the floor of the detention center got completely bloody. Several had their head broken and an ambulance had to be called
in to treat them.

At the detention center, the police interrogated us briefly
about our sex life and if we had even been "passive" [in anal
sex]. They then transferred us to the Esfahan Prison by a bus
that had only a window which was covered with a metal net.
Inside the bus was pitch black and they packed all of us, sev-
enty to eighty people, into it. The doors opened when we arrived at the prison and we were faced with a regiment of sol-
diers holding batons. There were a few high ranking officers
among them too. They began insulating and beating us as
soon as we got off the bus. We were then taken to an area
where we were given prison clothes and had our heads forcibly shaved with electric razors. This hurt us a lot...We were
given a numbered plaque to wear around our neck. They then
made us sit in front of this aperture, which we had to stare at,
and photographed us from various angles. After that, we were
taken to a large hall to be stripped naked and physically
searched... Eventually, we were put, in groups of fifteen to
sixteen, in cells that were built for only four persons. Most of
us had nowhere to sleep, and some of us slept on top of each
other... We were also put under immense psychological pressure... Everyone once in a while, a guard came to tell us to get

ready for our execution at 5 am of the next morning... Some of the guards threatened that they will put us in bags and throw us off a cliff... These abuses and pressures continued for about six days."[1]

During this period, many of the detainees were called in for interrogation and asked invasive questions regarding their private sexual life, in an attempt to obtain 'evidence' of same-sex sexual conduct. Ali told JFI & 6Rang:

"The interrogator wanted to know if I had ever had sexual intercourse. I told him that I had been raped once. He did not follow up with more questions about when and where that was. He wrote it down and then asked: "what were you up to after the party?" I said I was going to go home but he said: "No, you meant to do something else after the party. You were going to have sex, to engage in Lavat." I denied, "No sir! It was a simple birthday," but he put all the photographs they had collected from the guests' seized cameras in front of me, which showed the guests kissing and hugging and said "does this look like a simple birthday to you?" I said: "Sir, it is none of my business that the guests had dyed their hair and were kissing and hugging each other. They liked to do that and it is after all natural to hug and kiss other people. What is wrong with that? I know that this was just a birthday party. Now you want to insist that it was at a sex party, or something else..." Eventually, he asked me to sign a written statement, which included everything I had told him. This process of interrogation lasted for several days, during which the abuses and insults continued. We could not distinguish day and night from each other and did not know what sleeping and eating meant anymore."[2]

---

1 Interview with Ali, February 2011.

2 Interview with Ali, February 2011.

The detainees were also subjected to forced medical examinations by doctors of the Legal Medicine Organization of Iran (LMOI), in an attempt to find 'proof' of anal sex:

"One day we were told to get ready to go to the LMOI. We were all scared about why they want to take us there. At the LMOI office, we were photographed individually, and were each given a paper with our name and number on it. Inside a room, a doctor asked me to take off my pants and bend over. I was really embarrassed, and it was a truly difficult situation to endure. I felt the doctor used a projector lamp and pulled my cheeks apart to examine my butthole. He then asked me to get up and leave the room. They did the same thing to the others, and then we were all asked to wait in a hall with our hands handcuffed to each other in pairs. Then it was the turn for a psychiatrist to examine us. He asked me about my [sexual] identity and mental state. He also asked questions about my childhood. I told him that I liked to wear makeup ever since childhood. He did not ask a lot of questions and they were all of this nature. He wrote down a few things and asked me to leave. The other guys in our group were asked the same set of questions. We were not told About the results of our examinations, and whether they indicated that we had had sexual intercourse or not. We never found out."[1]

Of the 87 men arrested, 24 were eventually tried for "facilitating immorality and sexual misconduct" as well as possessing and drinking alcohol. In June 2007, an Esfahan court found all of them guilty of various combinations of these charges. However, except for three who were sentenced to up to 80 lashes for consumption of alcohol, the rest had their sentences reduced to fines of 10 million to 50 million riyals (US$1,000-5,000). The presiding judge recognized the detainees' "age" as well as their "affliction with a gender disorder" as mitigating factors warranting a reduced sentence.

---

1 Interview with Ali, February 2011.

3.2.2. Discrimination in Education

The findings of this report show that criminalization of sexual orientation and gender identity, together with the segregation of schools by gender, has had a deeply negative impact on access to secondary education. Lesbian, gay and transgender people frequently suffer harassment and beatings by school administrators as well as rape and violence perpetrated by other pupils. They are sometimes refused admission or expelled because of their real or perceived sexual orientation and gender identity, or forced to undergo sex reassignment surgeries as a condition to enroll. Akan, a 21 year-old female-to-male transgender, experienced discrimination and violence on a routine basis in his secondary school in Sanandaj. He told JFI & 6Rang:

> I was subjected to a lot of abuse in the school. The school authorities prevented me from participating in school activities with other students. They said I am a sexual pervert and have a corrupting effect on my classmates. I was not allowed to form friendships with others. I was a soccer player and I used to play in the premier league, but I was not allowed to take part in the school competitions. I was told that it was because I would corrupt the other students. I felt like a I am a prisoner. The school authorities always kept an eye on all my actions and friendships.[1]

Sayeh's Story

Sayeh, a lesbian woman, shared a similar experience of hostile and homophobic behavior by the school administration:

"Our high school vice principle used to give me a really hard time. She would look at me in a peculiar way, and never held

---

1 Interview with Akan, February 2011.

any respect for me. She even would talk all my friends out of befriending me. For example, she told them to not be friends with me or asked them what we did together. Once she deducted marks from a friend of mine who had persisted with our friendship in spite of the vice president's advice to end our friendship. She would also call my friends' mothers, and ask them to prohibit their daughters from befriending me.

Once I was spending time with one of my friends in the school's prayer hall…I remember being scared when she came up to us, because she always harassed me. She asked: "what are you two doing in here?" I said, "Nothing, we're just conversing." She asked, "only conversing?" and I responded, "yes." This is precisely what happened then: she started roaming the room and sniffing the air. The room was crowded with chairs and was very difficult to walk in. She then asked my friend to leave the room. I wanted to leave too, but she asked me to stay and said: "don't you dare think that I don't know about what the f* you're up to here! I am just waiting to catch you! And then I'll screw you over!" I was only sixteen or seventeen years old at the time. I told her that I had no idea what she was talking about. She then said, "We will see" and called me filthy names. Those were very difficult moments for me; she precisely wanted to know if we are physically intimate."[1]

For some lesbian, gay and transgender people, incidents of harassment and abuse reached a level of severity that they had no choice but to quit school. Farzam is a 22 year-old female-to-male transgender who experienced violence in his secondary school in Karaj. She told JFI & 6Rang:

> The school authorities called the police to the school on three separate occasions because I would refuse to wear the school uniforms that girls must wear in Iran. In grade ten, I had to change three high

---

1 Interview with Sayeh, September 2013.

schools, because my classmates would tell their parents about how I looked and the parents would immediately assume that I was a boy in disguise who meant to get close to their girls…The last time I went to school, my friends told me that the day before, the school had called the police on me again. As I was being told about this news in the school hallway, the principle suddenly appeared and took me to her office.

There was a den inside her office where the student files were kept. She pushed me inside there and began beating me while removing my clothes forcibly to find out how my body looked like. She said she wanted to know if I had a male or female body even though all my school records from grade one indicated that I was a girl. I was resisting this, crying and holding on tightly to my clothing so she could not remove them… She slapped me in the face and finally managed to open the buttons of my dress. I could only cry in response. When she saw that I had strapped my breasts, she let go of me. I was traumatized, and cannot recall what she exactly told me at that point time. I only remember her saying that I had to leave the school. Even though she saw my female body, I think she still suspected that I was an intersex. She asked for a doctor's note testifying that I was a girl. I did not go back to that school after this incident.[1]

Farzam's difficulties worsened after he started the process of sex reassignment. Because his appearance did not match his legal gender, he was accepted neither in girls' schools nor in boys'. He told JFI & 6Rang:

---

1 Interview with Farzam, September 2013.

I went to the ministry of education and begged them to register me at a school. I was a good student, and after three months of begging and crying, I finally managed to see the minister of education – as there was no one higher up than him. I was subsequently referred to a school in Tehran. They told me that because I wore men's clothes, they could not allow me to sit in a classroom with girls. I proposed that I study at home, and come back at a specified date to write my test at the school's office. They accepted my suggestion and proceeded to register me. The two women in the registration team asked me some very rude questions. This was enraging this but I had to answer their questions because my enrollment at the school depended on it. They asked me, for example, "what I have got down there and how it looks like?"

I studied for five or six months… and on the scheduled date; I arrived at the school early, eager and ready to take my examination. I was walking around by myself around the schoolyard when the janitor asked me to visit the principle's office. When I entered the office, the principle put my file on her table and informed me that I could not write the test anymore. I burst into tears and lost my speech. She did not explain the reason for her decision but I already figured from the way she had laid my file on the table that it was pointless to try to change her mind. I took my file and wandered aimlessly through the streets while crying. All those efforts, all those back and forth trips to the ministry of education ministry for three months had come to nothing.[1]

Farzam continued to experience harassment and discrimination in access to education after he completed the required

1 Interview with Farzam, September 2013.

sex reassignment procedures, because the information on his school records was not amended to match his new identification documents. He told JFI & 6Rang that he felt forced to leave school because of the harassment he experienced. Farzam is currently an asylum seeker in Turkey and is hoping to resume his studies after he is settled in a new country.

Students perceived as being lesbian, gay or transgender also experience widespread violence and harassment, including bullying and rape, from classmates, and school authorities rarely take any effective action to confront such prejudice and intimidation.[19]In an interview with JFI & 6Rang, Ali, a 29 year-old gay man, recalled that his school classmates subjected him to constant humiliation and harassment because they considered his behaviors and hand gestures to be "girly":

> The memories of those years are still fresh in my mind. My classmates always harassed and abused me. The abuses were not as serious as a beating but they slapped me on the face and followed me around to tease and taunt me. They would call me 'Miss Ali' or other names. At high school, they called me do jense because they said my hand gestures were like those of a girl… These insults, taunts and threats ultimately forced me to quit school in the last year of highschool. The school authorities used to repeatedly call me parents to school. There was a rumor going around that there is a boy in the school who is do jense, or from their perspective, hamjensbaz. This was despite the fact that I was super careful about how I acted. I tried to control my mannerisms but there was always something for them to find and make fun of.[1]

---

1 Interview with Ali, February 2011.

Pedram's Story

Pedram is a 24 year-old gay man who was raped on several occasions by his classmates because of his sexual orientation. He told JFI & 6Rang:

"When I was in grade eight, I expressed my feelings to a classmate, which ended up being a huge mistake. At the end of the school day, he and his friends stopped me in the street to rape me. I had thought he had the same feelings for me that I had for him but that was not true. The entire school had come to find out about me and everyone began jeering at me. My schoolmates threatened that if I did not agree to have sex with them, they would tell everyone in my neighborhood about me. I ended up giving in to their demands to the extent that I had become suicidal. They would rape me once every couple of weeks, sometimes in groups of five or six. I was so disturbed that, every now and then, I would climb our rooftop to contemplate suicide. I was not feeling well... I would escape school and hide in a movie theatre until my money ran out and I had to call my mom. My mother could not figure out what was going wrong and she would beg me to tell her what the problem was. She would often visit the school, and my teachers would tell her that I was not doing well in my studies. I had come to hate school. Ultimately, I told my mother about the situation and she changed my school."[1]

3.2.3. Abuse and Violence by Members of the Public

The laws that criminalize homosexual conduct and trans-gender expressions provide opportunities for abuse, including blackmail and extortion, of lesbian, gay and transgender people by members of the public. Amirali, an eighteen year-old female-to-male transgender told JFI & 6Rang about one of

---

1 Interview with Pedram, January 2013.

the incidents of violence and harassment he faced from a stranger in public, when he still dressed in women's clothes:

> I was in the metro when a woman stared at the way I was walking and accused me of being a female impersonator while directing insults and swear words at me. The police was called to the scene after a verbal argument broke out, and took me to the local police station. There, they told me that I must be strip searched so that my identity could be established.[1]

Hiva and her girlfriend, Nazanin, faced similar harassment after they were seen kissing by a stranger in the parking lot of a restaurant:

> Nazanin and I were kissing each other when a stranger saw us and began screaming and swearing. He called us hamjenbaz and threatened to call the police to come and arrest us. Staff and customers of the resultant all came on the scene and a fight broke out. Fortunately, we were regular customers at that restaurant and the owner knew us. So, he intervened in our favour and calmed the situation. We claimed that the man had made a mistake and was lying to cause us trouble. The police might have easily come and arrested us though if we were at a different place.[2]

According to the findings of JFI & 6Rang, taunts, insults and threats are a constant reality for lesbian, gay and transgender people and are in fact so common that many of them try to isolate themselves and avoid public interaction in order to reduce their risk of being harassed and abused. Faraz, a female-to-male transgender, told JFI & 6Rang:

---

1 Interview with Amirali, August 2013.

2 Interview with Hiva, January 2013.

> I got harassed on the street all the time. At the time, I wore men's clothing when I went out and had started taking hormones. My voice had not yet changed though and so I was ridiculed and insulted because of its high-pitched tone. This made me not want to talk. Whenever I opened my mouth to say something, strangers and friends said that my voice is like that of girls. People don't understand they don't have a right to device who I am.[1]

Sexual assault and other physical attacks against lesbian, gay and transgender people who do not conform to culturally approved models of femininity and masculinity are also all too common. Many of the lesbian, gay and transgender people interviewed by JFI & 6Rang reported that their life in Iran was marked by a constant fear of being assaulted and raped by men. This was particularly true for female-to-male transgender persons who had not undergone genital reassignment surgeries and worried about having their transgender identity unwantedly disclosed by men who try to fondle their genitals. Sohrab, a female-to-male transgender person, told JFI & 6Rang:

> Such unwanted [sexual] touching happens all the time. Fortunately, no one has ever found out about my [transgender] identity because I wear a fake penis. But the situation as a whole is very difficult. Levels of pressure are persistently high, bringing many transgender people to the edge of suicide… The situation would not be that different even if you put on women's clothing. You would still face similar risks of harassment and assault given how dirty-minded many men in Iran are.[2]

---

1 Interview with Faraz, January 2013.

2 Interview with Sohrab, January 2013.

During this research, JFI & 6Rang received seven accounts of sexual assault and rape, six of which were perpetrated by non-state actors. In all these cases, the victims said they not only did not feel protected by the law but also feared that they will be arrested and charged with sexual offences, if they were to file complaints with the police. This absence of an adequate police response to incidents of sexual assault and rape makes non-state actors feel emboldened to enact homophobic and transphobic violence with impunity, and is a source of human rights violation in that the state is failing in its duty to protect one group of its population from violence.

Ali's Story

"I have been raped on two occasions: The first incident was in 2004. My friend from high school Mohammad asked me to go with him to his house and help him fix his computer's speakers. At his house, I turned on his computer and realized that the speakers worked fine. As I came to tell him this, I saw a muscular boy entering the room. This boy held me up by my collar and said, "Move! Lie down on the floor." I asked what this was all about. As someone who had never experienced rape before, the idea of rape never even crossed my mind. I was shaking like a leaf, begging him to let me go but he wouldn't budge. He slapped me in face a couple of times and forcefully removed my clothes… They then both raped me and called me swear words. After some time, they allowed me to wear my clothes and leave the place. Despite feeling devastated, I did not know where to go or who to ask for help. I was afraid to go to the police. I feared that they may say I had asked to be raped myself and that instead of charging the offenders, they would accuse me of a crime. I had heard of such cases happening before.

When I arrived home that day, I cried for hours in my room and stayed home for a few days. I became severely depressed and began feeling weak and nauseous... I felt like I had no rights in my own country, absolutely no rights, and that I was treated like an animal."[1]

3.2.4. Abuse and Violence in the Family

A considerable number of lesbian, gay and transgender individuals interviewed by JFI & 6Rang, also reported being subjected to various forms of abuse by their family members because of their sexual orientation and gender identity. These included beatings and flogging as well as forms of psychological abuse such as enforced seclusion and isolation from friends and society, neglect and abandonment, verbal insults and death threats. For lesbians and female-to-male transgender persons, these abuses were often accompanied by threats or realities of being concerned into arranged marriage. Lesbian, gay and transgender individuals in Iran often have no recourse to justice or support for the abuse and violence they routinely suffer in their families, leading non-state actors to feel emboldened to enact homophobic and transphobic violence with impunity.

Soheil, a female-to-male transgender, told JFI & 6Rang that his father repeatedly beat him, forcing him to leave the family house at the end:

> My father was an extremely aggressive and ill-tempered man. He routinely beat me up with a belt. On several occasions, he got a knife and threatened to kill me. I was ultimately forced to leave the house. It was my family who actually told me to leave because they said they never wanted to see me again.[2]

---

1 Interview with Ali, February 2011.

2 Interview with Soheil, July 2012.

Rayan, who described herself as a "butch" lesbian, shared with JFI & 6Rang a similar experience of abuse and harassment from his brother:

> My brother would tell me that I was filthy and nothing but a piece of garbage. He would say I deserved to be beaten up because I had to be turned into a [normal] human. These insults damaged me so much emotionally that I did not even feel the physical pain anymore. I felt sorry for myself because I was being tortured for no reason. I did not understand why our brother-sister relationship could not be nicer. I felt sorry for my brother even more than I did for myself.[1]

Akan's Story

Akan, a 21 year-old female-to-male transgender, described to JFI & 6Rang the abuses he faced from his father because of his sexual orientation and gender identity:

"My father would tie my hands and legs, throw me into the bathroom, and whip me with his belt, because I did not dress like a girl. I do not understand how he could justify beating me just for not being able to fall in love with boys. He beat me all the time and I could not do any thing to stop that. I ultimately attempted suicide by slitting my wrists. When my father found me, he did not take me to the hospital because he did not want others to find out. He was trained in medicine and he stitched up my hand himself. Despite this, he continued to beat me and even threatened to kill me.

Towards the end of my stay in Iran, he told me that I would not be allowed to enroll in university unless I agreed to getting married. My parents were going to marry me off to an ac-

---

1 Interview with Rayan, August 2012.

quaintance. My father always said that I had been brainwashed into thinking that I was not a girl and that I am stop harboring these thoughts… I told him that I would set myself on fire if I was forced to marry but he did not listen and continued to go ahead with the marriage arrangement. This was when I decided to leave Iran."[1]

Iran is a signatory to the Convention on the Rights of the Child, which requires it to protect children from abuse and mistreatment, including at the hands of family members. Despite this obligation, Iranian authorities provide impunity to parents, especially fathers, who abuse their minor and adult children. Under Article 301 of the Islamic Penal Code, fathers are exempt from the punishment of *qesas* [retribution] if they murder their child.[2] In such cases, the Penal Codes provides for a prison sentence of three to ten years. Iranian laws also provide parents with considerable discretion in meting out physical punishment to their children. According Article 11179 of Iran's Civil Code, "parents have the right to punish their child, but they cannot punish their child in a manner that exceeds the norms of discipline."[3]

---

1 Interview with Akan, February 2011.

2 Islamic Penal Code of the Islamic Republic of Iran (2013) – Book II, online: http://rc.majlis.ir/fa/news/show/845002 (Retrieved on May 3, 2014).

3 Civil Code (1935), online: http://rc.majlis.ir/fa/law/show/92778 (Retrieved on May 3, 2014).

4. Legal Gender Recognition Procedures in Iran

Iran has been frequently described in domestic and international media as "a paradise for transsexual people." This might have been true in the late 80s when Iran was among one of the few nations in the world that allowed transgender individuals to change the gender marker on their official documents (including birth certificates, identity cards and passports) upon undergoing sex reassignment surgery. However, over a quarter of century later, Iran is no longer deserving of the praise. Its existing medical and legal procedures concerning transsexuality, which were set in motion as a result of Ayatollah Khomeini's *fatwa* in 1985, are wholly out of step with current best practice and understandings of Iran's obligations under international human rights law. Most egregiously, they require transgender individuals to alter their bodies through hormones and surgery and become permanently and irreversibly infertile in order to obtain the right to live their desired gender identity and sexual orientation, and obtain identity documents reflecting their gender identity. As noted in the preceding section, transgender individuals who transgress socially constructed gender expectations without applying to become diagnosed as "certified transsexuals" and undergoing sex reassignment surgery risk being identified as "homosexual," and targeted for discrimination, arbitrary arrest and detention, torture and other forms of ill-treatment.

As of the writing of this report, transgender individuals have to go through a maze of medical and legal institutions in order to obtain legal recognition of their gender on the basis of a series of ad hoc medical and administrative practices. These practices, which are often incoherent and unpredictable, give psychiatrists associated with the Legal Medicine Organization of Iran (LMOI) as well as administrative judges responsibility for issuance of new identity documents, at the center of decision-making. The processes of decision-making are not currently guided by a comprehensive legislation, and thereby vary from one city to another and indeed from one doctor and judge to the next.

Nevertheless, transgender people are generally required to complete four main steps in order to change their legal gender. These are: receiving a psychiatric diagnosis of "Gender Identity Disorder" from a psychiatrist; obtaining an official permit for sex change, provided by the Prosecution Office on the recommendation of LMOI; fulfilling a whole set of medical requirements, including hormone therapy, sterilization and genital reassignment surgeries; and applying to the court and the National Organization for Civil Registration to change their name and obtain new national identification documents reflecting their gender post-sex reassignment surgery. There is no legal certainty across the country as to the criteria that are applied in each of these steps. Many transgender individuals told JFI & 6Rang they considered the processes followed by psychiatrists and government officials to be arbitrary and in many instances invasive, degrading and based on gender stereotypes.

This chapter provides an overview of each of these steps in the arduous process of legal sex change and illustrates their adverse impact on the human rights of transgender people.

4.1. Background and Context

Legal gender recognition procedures in Iran are characterized by a fundamental dichotomy between concepts of perversion and deviation [*enheraf*] on the one hand and pathology and disorder [*ekhtelal*] on the other. Under this dichotomy, homosexual *deeds* are treated as crimes while homosexual *desires* are taken as symptoms of transsexualism. Acts of trans-dressing, which contest gender bipolarity, are prohibited, while surgical transitions that confirm gender bipolarity are promoted. Individuals who fail to conform to socially constructed gender expectations must therefore choose between being classified as "trans-patients" or "homo-perverts." The first label is assigned to individuals of diverse gender identities and sexual orientations, who commit to bring themselves, through hormone therapy, sterilization and genital reassignment surgery, within the bounds of gender "normalcy," while the second label is assigned to those who insist on expressing their experienced sexual orientation and gender identity without undergoing hormonal and surgical treatments.

The statements of Hujjat al-Islam Kariminia, a cleric who has written his dissertation on Islam and transsexuality, and who regularly comments in the domestic media on the subject, are highly emblematic in this regard. In his speeches, Kariminia repeatedly states that, "Islam has a cure for people suffering from this problem [Gender Identity Disorder]. If they want to change their gender, the path is open." He always makes sure to clarify, however, that "this discussion is fundamentally separate from a discussion regarding homosexuals. Absolutely not related. Homosexuals are doing something unnatural and against religion…It is clearly stated in our Islamic law that such behavior is not allowed because it disrupts the social order."[1]

Referring to what he calls a "Great Wall of China" between "homo-perverts" and "trans-patients," Kariminia explains:

> [T]ransexuals are discontent with their sexual/gender selves, and they are not necessarily hamjensbaz even though a few of them may engage in this filthy activity… the majority of them desire to have a legal and Shar'ia life… This is confirmed by medical sciences, which also separate the two categories by noting that a hamjensbaz has no problem with his/her body, is not unhappy with his/her body. He believes he is a man and goes after doing this filthy [kasif] act; she believes she is a

---

1 Vanessa Barford, "Iran's Diagnosed transsexuals," BBC News (25 February 2008), online: http://news.bbc.co.uk/1/hi/world/middle_east/7259057.stm (Retrieved on May 4, 2014).

woman and engages in this ugly [zisht] act ... These acts are against the Shari'a, against public order, thus they are sinful and if a crime is proven, it is punishable.[1]

When asked about the possibility of trans-dressing and adopting a non-surgical transgender identity, Kariminia states:

There were people in the past who were passing themselves off as women and there were women who tried to pass themselves off as men. It is clearly stipulated in our Islamic law that such behavior is not allowed because it violates moral rules and disrupts social order.[2]

The discourse of Iranian officials is replete with statements such as the one made by Karimina, all of which warn against confounding transsexuality and homosexuality. According to a briefing issued by the Education and Research Bureau of the Islamic Republic of Iran Broadcasting (IRIB),

There are still a lot of people in our society who believe that transsexuals are *hamjensbaz* because they are not familiar with who Gender Identity Disorder patients are and how they are different from sexual perverts such as *hamjensbaz* people. Another factor that must be kept in sight is the stance that Internet websites, operated by groups that oppose the Islamic Republic of Iran, take toward this issue. By depicting the difficulties of transsexual patients in Iran, and offering a series of psychological and societal constructions pertaining to their plights – and thereby commanding public sympathy toward their circumstances – these websites attempt to cleanse the incorrigible image of homosexuals and bisexuals who are com-

---

1 Afsaneh Najmabadi, Professing Selves: Transsexuality and Same-Sex Desire in Contemporary Iran (Duke University Press, 2014).

2 *Be Like Others*, DVD. Directed by Tanaz Eshaghian. Iran, Canada, U.S.: Wolfe Video, 2008. This segment of Kariminia's speech is available online via https://www.youtube.com/watch?v=GZPkM2fZ_vc (min. 00:59)

pletely reprehensible and rejected under our religious principles and beliefs. This problem demands that producers of culture remain cautious and work to promote and ensure the natural rights of transsexual and intersex patients while preventing defenders of sexual perverts from taking advantage of these efforts. The authorities must further ensure that confronting cases of sexual perversion will not result in violations of the basic rights of Gender Identity Disorder patients.[1]

The dichotomization of gender variant and sexual minority individuals along these lines has opened up a possibility for bestowing legal recognition upon transsexuals as *dojenseh* [bi-sexed] patients who are on the path of fitting into a proper gender location. This has not, however, challenged the deep-seated homophobia and transphobia that characterizes the Iranian legal framework on sexual orientation and gender identity. On the contrary, it has engendered new methods for reinforcing gender stereotypes and forms of homophobic and transphobic prejudice that contribute to the legal and social exclusion of lesbian, gay and transgender people, violating their human dignity and personal integrity.

As will be explained in this chapter, medical and judicial authorities frequently misapply, with the consent and acquiescence of the government, the term Gender Identity Disorder to individuals with homosexual feelings and transgender identities, and condition their right to express their preferred gender identity and sexual orientation on undergoing surgeries which frequently result in irreversible sterility and debilitating medical complications. Transgender individuals who do not apply to become diagnosed as "certified transsexuals" and undergo sex reassignment surgery risk getting identified as "homosexual" and targeted for discrimination and violence.

---

1 The Education and Research Bureau of the Islamic Republic of Iran Broadcasting "Gender Disorders (Transsexuals)" (prepared by Mohammad Ali Ganji), 22 June 2008, p.14.

4.2. Psychiatric Diagnosis

Obtaining an official permit for sex change is a prerequisite for adopting dress and mannerisms of one's own experienced gender without facing a risk of arrest and conviction for transdressing, accessing specific treatments such as hormone therapy or sex reassignment surgeries, qualifying for modest financial assistance from Iran's State Welfare Organization, obtaining identity documents reflecting one's gender, and applying for exemption from military service (for male-to-female transgenders). In order to receive this life-changing permit, transgender individuals must undergo between eight to twelve psychotherapy sessions, along with hormonal and chromosomal tests, with a view to obtaining a medical statement that diagnoses them with "Gender Identity Disorder" and recommends them for sex reassignment surgery to the judiciary.

Depending on their financial situation, transgender individuals complete these psychotherapy sessions either with private psychiatrists who have established a working relation with the LMOI or with publicly funded psychiatrists at the Tehran Psychiatric Institute (TPI), a clinic affiliated with the Iran University of Medical Sciences. At TPI, the diagnostic process begins with a four to six month period of psychotherapy with a TPI-affiliated psychiatrist, and ends with an interview with a Determination Commission composed of between three to five mental health professionals. Upon the completion of this process, the TPI decides whether to recommend an applicant for sex reassignment surgery to the LMOI, require further tests and therapy or reject the applicant altogether.

Once the TPI or a private psychiatrist recommends an applicant for sex reassignment surgery, he or she can present to the Prosecution Office to apply for an official permit for a sex change. The Office of the General Prosecutor in turn refers the applicant to the Psychiatrist Ward of the LMOI, which then takes control of the process and sets an interview with a Commission of psychiatrists and clinical psychologists working under its auspices. This Commission is charged with determining the applicant's "affliction with Gender Identity Disorder" and confirming his/her eligibility for undergoing hormone therapy and sex reassignment surgery.

The transgender people with whom JFI & 6Rang spoke generally agreed on the importance of having medical supervision prior to and while accessing hormone therapy and sex reassignment surgeries. They were also in favor of getting affirmative psychological support and counseling from psychologists who specialized in gender issues. However, many of them did not consider the process of psychiatric diagnosis described above to be supportive or therapeutic. They reported feeling anxious in sessions with mental health professionals, and under pressure to conform to gender stereotypes inconsistent with their actual gender identity needs or self-identity. Pressure is imposed by the fact that the diagnosis of "Gender Identity Disorder" is the only one that enables individuals to trans-dress, access health treatments, and ultimately receive legal gender recognition.

Soheil, one of the first female-to-male transsexual persons to receive his diagnosis from the TPI in the early 2000s, discusses the feelings of distress and disbelief that he experienced throughout the diagnostic process as follows:

> You have to attend ten sessions of "therapy," during which you are provided with no information or counseling and are only grilled with questions. They leave no energy for you. You talk and talk and they take notes...At the end of these sessions, you are asked to leave and return in five months. Over the course of these five months, you remain anxious about what they are going to decide. You return in five months to answer another round of questions, this time before a Commission of several doctors and medical students. These are some of their questions. "Since when did you realize you are like this?

What's going to happen if you have an operation? What will happen if you don't have an operation? What is your motivation for having an operation? What is your occupation right now? Do you always dress like boys when you go out?" You can be dishonest and give canned answers to these questions. They ask what happens if you can't undergo an operation and you say I will kill myself. They ask what happens if you can receive an operation and you say it will be great. At the end of this process, they give you a date to return and collect their decision. This decision, if positive, states: "Person X is afflicted with Gender Identity Disorder. We recommend him or her to the Legal Medicine Organization for the next step." You then have to go to the Legal Medicine Organization and answer the same set of questions again.[1]

Many transgender individuals told JFI & 6Rang that their diagnostic process was based on unfounded gender stereotypes that do not necessarily apply to all transgender people. Female-to-male transgender persons felt that they had to cut their hair short, stop wearing make-up, wear baggy or stereotypically masculine clothing and act like a macho man in order to be perceived as trans. Conversely, male-to-female transgender persons felt that they had to wear excessive make-up, express an interest in household activities like cooking, sowing, ironing and cleaning, appear emotional and submissive, and enact other outdated stereotypes about femininity.

Transgender people who do not identify according to the binary male-female divide run a risk of not being accepted as transgender, which excludes them from accessing legal recognition of their gender. Accordingly, an active blog called Trans-e Gomnam [Anonymous Trans], in which transgender people share their questions, concerns and experiences, ad-

---

1 Interview with Soheil, July 2012.

vises "female-to-male transgender persons to appear as masculine looking as possible (and male-to-female transgender
persons as feminine looking as possible) when presenting to
their LMOI appointments." Ali Rad, a female-to male transsexual who actually prepares applicants for their TPI and
LMOI interviews, told JFI & 6Rang:

> To establish one's transsexuality, the doctors take a
> number of key factors into account that I do not
> hold as valid whatsoever. For example, in terms of
> visual appearance, they look for headscarves, loose
> gowns, baggy pants, sneakers, and rough appearances
> – which can, in truth, be the look of quite a lot of
> people. It is all very hilarious. I do not know how to
> make these people understand that their simplistic at-
> titude actually ridicules my identity as a female-to-
> male transsexual. In order to diagnose female-to-
> male transsexuals, these doctors take as symptomatic
> things like having sexual relationship with women
> and assuming a top or active role in sex...Trivial and
> transitory things like one's choice of dress and make-
> up cannot be an accurate indication of one's iden-
> tity...But the doctors have turned such things into
> checkboxes based on which they assign someone a
> permit for sex reassignment. To give you an ironic
> example: they rejected a friend of mine who is truly a
> female-to-male transsexual because he could not
> wear what was considered masculine clothing to the
> interview. At the time, he still had a womanly phy-
> sique and he could not hide it well under men's
> clothing. So he was afraid of walking out in the
> streets with a woman's body dressed in men's cloth-
> ing. But he got turned down...The second time, we
> found a safe way for him to come to the interview in

masculine clothing. They accepted him on the spot. The whole process is this simple and absurd. [1]

Transgender individuals interviewed by JFI & 6Rang believed that the diagnostic criteria on which mental health professionals rely are not transparent, and reported intrusive queries about their sexual orientation, sexual practices and sexual fantasies. Sohrab, a twenty-seven-year-old female-to-male transgender person, said:

> I am not sure what to call my therapist's questions: ridiculous? Terrible? Scandalous or what? Just imagine. It is your first or second session with a therapist and she suddenly turns to you and asks about your wet dreams: "How do you have sex in your dreams? Have you ever seen a penis in reality or in your dreams, and what did it look like? If you have never seen it in reality, how does it look like in your dreams? What was your sex/gender in your sexual dreams?" These are the sorts of questions that I doubt anyone would have any concrete answers for… and I think they are actually quite irrelevant to the process of diagnosis and treatment. [2]

In many instances, transgender applicants were asked such invasive questions about their private and intimate life in the presence of their parents, which made the process of scrutiny more abusive and degrading. Soheil said:

> One of my female-to-male transsexual friends, who was about thirty-five years old, was asked to bring his father along on his visit to the Legal Medicine Organization. And in front of his old father, the Commission asked questions about his sexual life, and

1 Interview with Ali Rad, August 2012.
2 Interview with Sohrab, January 2013.

more specifically how he had sex with girls. He had
mentioned that he was not comfortable to discuss
these matters in the presence of his father. The
Commission nevertheless insisted that he needed to
talk about how he had sex with girls if he maintained
that he was a man. [1]

According to current practices, the LMOI requires every
transgender applicant to bring his/her parents to the final
Commission interview and secure his consent to sex reassignment surgery. Individuals cannot receive a permit for sex
change and undergo sex reassignment surgeries if their parents do not give consent. In addition to violating the right to
privacy, this requirement compromises the right of adult
transgender applicants to access the health treatments they
wish on the basis of free, informed consent. Transgender individuals interviewed by JFI & 6Rang were often very critical
of this requirement. Sohrab told JFI & 6Rang:

> LMOI officials will issue the applicant the permis-
> sion right then and there if the parents say that they
> "have no problem with their child undergoing sex
> reassignment surgery" and that they "understand
> their child has a problem." They refuse to allow the
> operation however if the parents say, "we do not
> want our child to be operated on." They ask the ap-
> plicant to return in four months… For them, the
> most important criterion is the family's consent. So
> what becomes of the person who wants to be oper-
> ated on but cannot get the family's consent? And…
> what does this say about the relevance of the psy-
> chiatrist's diagnosis? If that is their criterion, then
> why not just take the parents along, and head straight
> to the hospital for the operation from the very be-
> ginning? Why won't the father just sign a paper that
> says 'he accepts his child to remove her breast and

1 Interview with Soheil, July 2012.

uterus and then be done with this entire process? Why put people through this year-long ordeal at all, and, meanwhile, charge them so much money? [1]

In 2013, the LMOI announced that it had updated its criteria of Gender Identity Disorder diagnosis. The criteria are not, however, publicly accessible and JFI & 6Rang has not been able to learn what behaviors and qualities are included. Nevertheless, accounts of individuals who have gone through the diagnostic process suggest that LMOI-affiliated mental health professionals frequently emphasize social gender non-conformity and same-sex sexual orientation over actual Gender Identity Disorder, defined in DSM-V (where it is listed as Gender Dysphoria) as chronic distress with one's physical sex characteristics. Farnaz, a twenty-seven-year-old lesbian woman who sought to obtain an official sex change permit in order to circumvent strict gendered dress codes, explains how she received her diagnosis of Gender Identity Disorder:

> I told them that I had no desire to live with men: "I like women, I like to be with them, and I don't want to wear the headscarf and gown. I have hated skirts since I was a child, and I never liked playing with dolls." These were my responses to the types of questions they asked about my childhood and how I realized to be different from others. Their questions were general and so were answers. "Have you slept with a woman before?" I said yes. "How was it?" I said it was great. I even told them that I do not have a problem with the body I had. I just did not want to dress the way women are expected dress. [2]

Solmaz meanwhile notes that her girlfriend in Shiraz was encouraged by her psychiatrist to undergo sex reassignment sur-

---

1 Interview with Sohrab, January 2013.

2 Interview with Farnaz, April 2012.

gery merely on account of her same-sex sexual orientation and
without any noted preference for trans-dressing:

> The situation in Shiraz was quite ridiculous. My girl-
> friend, who was actually very "feminine," was told by
> her doctor that she could get a diagnosis from him
> with which she could apply to undergo sex reassign-
> ment surgery. I was shocked and could not just be-
> lieve the basis on which the doctor had made this
> statement. What would happen to someone who is
> clueless if she is given such a diagnosis? My girlfriend
> wore feminine-clothing styles and make-up and she
> was advised to change her sex just because she had
> informed her doctor of her attraction toward
> women. [1]

According to Fariba, mental health professionals take homosexual orientation as symptomatic of "Gender Identity Disorder." The corollary of this is that they do not endorse the
medical "creation" of post-operative homosexuals. While she
plans on self-identifying as lesbian after her male-to-female
sex reassignment surgery, she says:

> I did not make any mention of my attraction to
> women in my therapy sessions. I knew that I had to
> say that I am attracted toward men in order to get
> their permission for sex reassignment operation. [2]

The foregoing practices run afoul of contemporary treatment
protocols across the world in which "sexual attraction (sexual
orientation) per se plays only a minor role."[3] This is, for example, reflected in the Standards of Care issued by the
WPATH in 2011, which do not mention the term sexual ori-

---

1 Interview with Solmaz, July 2013.

2 Interview with Fariba, March 2014.

3 Gender Identity Disorder Sub-Workgroup of the DSM-V Task Force, "Memo Outlining Evidence for Change for Gender Identity Disorder in the DSM-5" (20130) 42 *Arch
Sex Behav* 901, pp. 906-907.

entation or sexual attraction even once, "suggesting a contemporary consensus that sexual orientation or sexual attraction is of minimal importance to treatment providers."[1] It is also noticeable in current DSM-IV-TR diagnostic criteria, which has eliminated the specifier pertaining to sexual attraction (sexual orientation).

In labeling individuals with gender variant identities and expressions as having a "mental disorder," diagnostic practices prevalent in Iran also disregard efforts to depathologize gender non-conformity, and to exclude members of the transgender community who are not anatomically dysphoric, and who neither seek nor desire medical or surgical intervention to change their bodies from the DSM diagnostic criteria. In 2010, the WPATH, in urging the worldwide depathologization of gender non-conformity, stated: "The expression of gender characteristics, including identities, that are not stereotypically associated with one's assigned sex at birth is a common and culturally diverse human phenomenon [that] should not be judged as inherently pathological or negative."[2]

4.3. Hormone Therapy

Broadly speaking, hormone therapy refers to medical procedures intended to introduce hormones associated with the gender that a transgender person self-identifies with. Some hormone-induced changes such as those involving the use of hormones to delay the effects of puberty are fully reversible. Others are, however, either completely irreversible (e.g.

---

1 World Professional Association for Transgender Health, "Standards of Care for the Health of Transsexual, Transgender and Gender Non Conforming People," Seventh Version (2012), online:
http://www.wpath.org/uploaded_files/140/files/Standards%20of%20Care,%20V7%20 Full%20Book.pdf (Retrieved on 4 May 2014).

2 WPATH, World Professional Association for Transgender Health, Board of Directors, *WPATH De-Psychopathologisation Statement* (2010), online:
http://tgmentalhealth.com/2010/05/26/wpath-releases-de-psychopathologisation-statement-on-gender-variance/ (Retrieved on May 3, 2014).

changes in vocal cords, such as deepening of the voice caused by testosterone) or only partially reversible (e.g. gynaecomastia caused by estrogens).[1] Hormone therapy is an essential element in any real-life test for individuals considering sex reassignment surgery and it plays an important role in helping transgender individuals experience a sense of psychological and emotional fulfillment.

In Iran, transgender individuals are not allowed by law to access hormone therapy until the LMOI diagnoses them as suffering from "Gender Identity Disorder" and issues them with a permit for sex reassignment. However, large numbers of transgender individuals administer hormone therapy prior to applying for a permit because they believe that this can increase their chances of success before the LMOI. Mehran, who has initiated hormone therapy without an official permit, says:

> My friends have recommended that I change my looks before appearing in front of the Commission because those who sit on that Commission judge a book by its cover. Also, this presents my family with a fait accompli, which might force them into helping me… This approach worked for my friend and he was able to get his permit very quickly.[2]

Transgender people frequently resort to self-medication or seek out unscrupulous hormone providers because they cannot locate or afford medical practitioners familiar with gender identity issues. Kia is a female-to-male transsexual person who self-administered hormones for two years before he started his sex reassignment procedures. He told JFI & 6Rang:

---

1 World Professional Association for Transgender Health, "Standards of Care for the Health of Transsexual, Transgender and Gender Non Conforming People," Seventh Version (2012), p. 27, online:
http://www.wpath.org/uploaded_files/140/files/Standards%20of%20Care,%20V7%20Full%20Book.pdf (Retrieved on 4 May 2014).

2 Interview with Mehran, November 2013.

> I started my hormone therapy in 2002. In those
> years, no physician would agree to treat transsexual
> patients. It is only in the past few years that things
> have begun to change. During my time the doctors
> would avoid transsexuals, and even barred them
> from entering their office. Hormone therapy special-
> ists refused to give consultation to transsexual pa-
> tients.

In contrast, now that I live here in Europe, I have an auto-
matic check-up every six months. They check my hormones,
send me the prescription, and my pharmacy is obligated to
provide me with the medicine. Over here, a transsexual person is treated like a human being, whereas in Iran I know
transsexual people are desperate to find hormones. This was
my situation when I still lived in Iran: I had to pretend that I
had breast cancer and needed testosterone for that reason…I
had done all this research to come up with a right excuse and
identified a pharmacy that was willing to provide me with
such hormones. Not all transsexuals were able to do the same
and they were forced to buy it from the black market.[1]

Faraz is another female-to-male transsexual who obtained
non-prescribed hormone medication:

> I began doing hormone therapy on my own. I would
> get the shots from my friend who was also a trans-
> sexual. His father worked at the National Iranian Oil
> Company and his workplace medical insurance cov-
> ered the cost of some medications. He would get
> cheap hormones and give them to me, as he himself
> would not inject Iranian-made hormones. I would
> get the cheap shots and inject them once every week.
> I had not yet had undergone an operation at that
> time… My friend was concerned that I was getting
> sick, and warned me that he would stop giving me

---

1 Interview with Kia, October 2013.

the hormones. I listened to him and reduced the in-
jections to once every three weeks.[1]

Every transgender person to whom JFI & 6Rang spoke noted
that self-medication has resulted in the use of excessive doses
of hormones among members of the transgender community,
causing a range of adverse and undesirable side effects including, but not limited to: Weight gain, fatigue, mood changes,
high blood pressure, liver disease and heart disease. Soheil
told JFI & 6Rang:

> A lot of our transsexual friends have chosen to do
> hormone therapy on their own because they lack the
> support of their families and the financial means to
> visit a doctor. I am one of those people. It has been
> thirteen years since I last visited a doctor for hor-
> mone therapy. Back then, when I started my own
> hormone therapy, I would inject more than 1000cc
> of hormones per week in order to speed up the re-
> sults and change the appearance of my face. The rec-
> ommended limit is 100cc per week. I have ended up
> developing a lot of health problems as a result of this
> practice: Blood pressure, liver and kidney problems,
> obesity, bone pain, and many other health complica-
> tions that I do not know the name of because of my
> insufficient medical knowledge.[2]

Many transgender people in Iran rush into hormone therapy
in order to bring their body in line with an intended masculine
or feminine presentation, and to circumvent mandatory dress
codes that restrict their freedom to dress and appear in public
in conformity with the gender with which they identify rather
than the gender that was assigned to them at birth. This much
sought-after freedom comes, however, at a great cost for
transgender individuals who administer hormone therapy

1 Interview with Faraz, January 2013.
2 Interview with Soheil, July 2012.

without pursuing sex reassignment procedures, as they have to bear identification documents that manifestly contradict their appearance and gender identity.

As will be later explained in greater detail, the lack of identification exposes transgender individuals to widespread discrimination in areas such as employment, education, health care and access to goods and services, and subjects them to serious risks of harassment and violence, including at the hands of state officials. In this respect, Arman, a female-to-male transgender person, told JFI & 6Rang:

> Some female-to-male transgender persons are over-weight, and no matter how short they cut their hair, one can still tell that they are women. And mind you, we are speaking of a person who has grown a beard and whose voice has changed, but, nevertheless, continues to have a female body. This is why it is very easy for the authorities to tell them apart in the streets and arrest them, and why they need to proceed with sex reassignment procedures and carry a permit so as to prove that they can walk around without hijab.[1]

Such risks of arrest and abuse constitute a major source of stress and anxiety for transgender people, contribute to their social isolation and ostracization, and compel many of them to ultimately opt for sex reassignment surgery in order to obtain new identification documents reflecting their gender expression and identity. According to Arman,

> There is no going back after you begin hormone therapy. Your beard grows, and your voice changes. At the beginning, you may shave your beard and get away with pretending to have a sore throat. But this excuse cannot last forever, and eventually people in

---

1 Interview with Arman, June 2013.

your former gendered environment would take notice of the changes and ask for your removal. Your
changing appearance would simply make your continued presence in the former circles impossible, and
eventually you would be forced to leave them. If you
are not part of one gender group, you have to try to
get into the other, which leaves you with no choice
but to go ahead with sex reassignment surgery. Hormone therapy is the end of everything: It is like a
bridge that burns down soon after you cross it.[1]

4.4. Sex Reassignment Surgeries and Change
of Legal Documents

As stated above, transgender people in Iran cannot obtain
legal recognition of their gender unless they undergo sex reassignment surgeries and irreversible sterilization. This entails
the removal of breasts (mastectomy), uterus (hysterectomy),
ovaries (oophorectomy) and fallopian tubes (salpingectomy)
for female-to-male candidates, and testicles (orchiectomy) and
penis (penectomy) for male-to-female candidates. Since the
kind of surgical treatments required for legal gender recognition are not codified in law, courts sometimes require addi-
tional procedures such as the creation of a neo-phallus (phalloplasty) and testicular implant surgeries. Mohsen is a female-
to-male transsexual who was denied legal gender recognition
because he failed to receive phalloplasty. He wrote on the
blog Trans-e Gomnam:

> The judge reviewing my case sent me to the Legal
> Medicine Organization for a physical examination. I
> went to the branch that was located in Vanaq Square.
> Over there, two men and five women examined me.
> First, they inspected my beard and asked how long I

---

1 *Ibid.*

have had it. They then turned to my breasts. Luckily Dr. Oskooyi had done a good job on my breasts and they thought I had never operated on them and they were always so flat. I was then sent to Imam Khomeini Hospital to get them the entire file on my uterus and ovaries removal operation. I did, and when I returned, they asked me to pull down my pants to inspect my genitals. I asked if it was possible for them to not go through with this inspection, but they refused, indicating that if I did not cooperate they would refuse to write me the required letter. I pulled down my pants with embarrassment. They took a look and said in a disappointed voice that my genitals are womanly. They then asked me to leave the room and pick up my letter downstairs. I tried to explain to them why I was not yet in a position to receive a genital reassignment surgery but they were much too cruel to pay my explanations any heed.

I took the sealed letter they gave me to the court. It felt like a hundred pound sledge struck my head when I realized what the letter said. It read, "Mastectomy, hysterectomy and oophorectomy have been completed but the sex organ is still feminine in appearance." There was no mention of how large my clitoris had grown. The judge ruled that all the required steps for sex reassignment have not been satisfied and new identification documents would not be issued. [1]

Mazdak, another female-to-male transsexual had a similar experience. Being a resident of Germany, he was able to change the gender marker on his German identification documents after he underwent a hysterectomy and mastectomy. He was

---

[1] The weblog Trans-e-Gomnam (Anonymous Trans) was hacked in 2012 by unidentified assailants. JFI & 6Rang were however able to recover the data of the blog, including the posts cited in this report.

not, however, able to change the legal gender on his Iranian passport because he did not wish to undergo genital reassignment surgery. His mother told JFI & 6Rang:

> The Iranian Embassy refused to issue him a passport with his male name, because he did not wish to undergo genital reassignment surgery. The officials told us that obtaining a male sex organ is a must. This is while he has already gone through all the legal steps of changing his name and legal gender in Germany, and has received a new passport. [1]

There is no legal certainty across Iran as to the criteria applied by different courts for legal gender recognition. Some accept the validity of medical certificates that attest to the fact that the individual meets the required hormone therapy and sex reassignment conditions. Others require intrusive and degrading physical examinations by court-appointed examiners. A number of transgender individuals told JFI & 6Rang that they had to refer to several courts before they could confirm their eligibility for new identification documents. This is how a female-to-male transsexual identified as "M." shared his ordeal on the blog, Trans-e Gomnam:

> In 2011, I applied for an identification card in my hometown. After suffering from a lot of humiliation at the hands of the clerks and secretaries working in the court, I managed to submit my file to the judge. I was told that I had to wait for two months for my turn but I could write a request and have it signed by the judge presiding over the branch in order to fast track my file. So I wrote the letter and visited the judge for his signature. I handed him the certificate that the Legal Medicine Organization had issued but he said: "you had no physical problems prior to your sex change operation, and your issues were strictly

---

1 Interview with Nasrin (Mazdak's mother), May 2012.

psychological. If I allow for this request, then just about anyone can apply for a sex change." He therefore turned down my case. I was sure that this judge would never rule in my favor so I decided to come to Tehran and apply from there. [1]

Raham's note on the blog Trans-e Gomnam confirms Mohsen's experience. He writes:

Iranian judges are free to rule as they please and no one can question them for this. This is precisely why the processes followed by courts are arbitrary and our sex reassignment cases are ruled subjectively... Some judges accept the surgeon's note while others decide to rely on the opinion of the Legal Medicine Organization. Unfortunately, in the latter situation, female-to-male candidates face the requirement that they undergo testicular implant surgery. This is because of the internal bylaws of the Legal Medicine Organization. If you do not wish to undergo this operation, you will have to close your case and refer to a different branch where the judge does not require you to obtain an opinion from the Legal Medicine Organization. [2]

In addition to being critical of the arbitrary criteria applied by courts, transgender individuals have raised concerns that they are commonly forced to submit to unprofessional and humiliating physical examinations by judges and government officers who are not authorized by law to conduct physical examinations. This is how Leila, a male-to-female transsexual, recounted her experience of being asked to undress in front of the judge deciding her case:

---

1 The weblog Trans-e-Gomnam (Anonymous Trans) was hacked in 2012 by unidentified assailants. JFI & 6Rang wew however able to recover the data of the blog, including the posts cited in this report.

2 The weblog Trans-e-Gomnam (Anonymous Trans) was hacked in 2012 by unidentified assailants. JFI & 6Rang were however able to recover the data of the blog, including the posts cited in this report.

Ayatollah Raazini would always ask us to pull down our pants and underwear so he could see the difference between our sex organ and that of an ordinary woman. He would begin by asking questions to invite our trust, only to say at once: "pull it down so I can see the difference between yours and that of an ordinary woman." We would tell him about the differences between an ordinary woman's sex organ and ours...and showed him our genitals, hoping that he would not subject us to creepy gazes and sexually offensive comments, and understand our problem. [1]

Kaveh, a female-to-male transsexual, shared a similar experience:

When I went to register for a new identity card, I was asked to undergo physical examination. I told them: "my medical documents state that I have had an operation on my breasts and I have had a hysterectomy, and I am telling you that I have not received genital reassignment surgery. What is it then that you want to see?" The women in charge did not however listen to me and insisted that they had to inspect my genitals. I finally gave up and said: "ok you want to see it? Here, come and take a look." [2]

Transgender individuals who manage to establish that they have fulfilled the required medical treatments are referred to the National Organization for Civil Registration (NOCR) to apply for a new birth certificate and national identity card reflecting their gender identity. It is based on these documents that they can subsequently apply for other identification documents, such as passport and driving license, or request duplicate diplomas and professional certifications. A number of cases reported to JFI & 6Rang suggest, however, that some

---

1 Interview with Leila, March 2012.

2 Interview with Kaveh, January 2013.

courts order the NOCR to indicate the former name and gender marker of the transgender individual seeking legal gender recognition on the last page of the birth certificate followed by a statement that the individual has undergone sex reassignment procedures. This "involuntary outing" constitutes a major concern for transgender individuals as they are forced to give up aspects of their right to privacy whenever they are asked to produce their birth certificate in order to obtain goods or services, find employment, enroll in education, obtain housing, or claim welfare benefits.

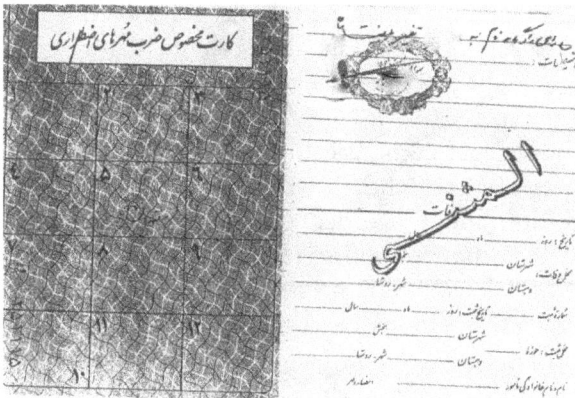

A duplicate birth certificate revealing the previous gender of the document holder

As of the writing of this report, transgender individuals who do not want to, or for health or financial reasons cannot, undergo sex reassignment surgeries are excluded from obtaining documents that correspond to their gender identity and gender expression and they are exposed to widespread discrimination. Some like M. have been discriminated against in finding employment:

> I find many good job positions, but all of them require an identification card to be hired. Right now, I am working at an acquaintance's company, but I have no salary, because the company's bankrupt. They have given a room in which I get to spend my nights comfortably and without the fear of being harassed. In return, I take care of some of their of-

fice work. I thank God because this is still a lot better than sleeping on a park bench.[1]

Others like Farzam have been denied permission to enroll in school because they do not have identification documents reflecting their gender identity and gender expression:

> I went to the ministry of education and begged them to register me at a school. I was a good student, and after three months of begging and crying, I finally managed to see the minister of education – as there was no one higher up than him. I was subsequently referred to a school in Tehran. They told me that because I wore men's clothes, they could not allow me to sit in a classroom with girls. I proposed that I study at home, and come back at a specified date to write my test at the school's office. They accepted my suggestion and proceeded to register me. The two women in the registration team asked me some very rude questions. This was enraging this but I had to answer their questions because my enrollment at the school depended on it. They asked me, for example, "what I have got down there and how it looks like?"

> I studied for five or six months…and on the scheduled date, I arrived at the school early, eager and ready to take my examination. I was walking around by myself around the schoolyard when the janitor asked me to visit the principle's office. When I entered the office, the principle put my file on her table and informed me that I could not take the test anymore. I burst into tears and lost my speech. She did not explain the reason for her decision but I already figured from the way she had laid my file on the table

1 The weblog Trans-e-Gomnam (Anonymous Trans) was hacked in 2012 by unidentified assailants. JFI & 6Rang were however able to recover the data of the blog, including the posts cited in this report.

that it was pointless to try to change her mind. I took my file and wandered aimlessly through the streets while crying. All those efforts, all those back and forth trips to the ministry of education ministry for three months had come to nothing.[1]

4.5. Exemption from Military Service

Under Iranian law, all males above the age of eighteen are required to serve a mandatory military service of 20 months. There are, however, certain exceptions for those who cannot service on account of physical or mental health problems or disabilities. Until a few years ago, transsexuality was considered to be "a moral and sexual deviancy" warranting exemption from compulsory military service, as per Article 33, Paragraph 8 of the regulatory code that governs medical exemptions. In August 2001, as a result of numerous efforts made by transsexual activists, the stated grounds of exemption by reason of "transsexuality" was changed to "medical endocrinal disease." This change, which was fairly positive, was coupled with a troubling one changing the nature of military exemptions granted to transsexuals from permanent to temporary. As a result of this latter change, transsexuals are now granted exemption for a period of six months during which they must take the necessary steps to undergo sex reassignment surgeries. Transsexual individuals who fail to comply with this requirement cannot renew their exemption certificates. According to Mohammad, a transsexuals' rights activist,

> The change is because of the fact that many transsexuals who receive exemption permits never undergo surgery. Through this new policy, the authorities are trying to lower the number of permit holders. When I first heard about this new policy, I got ex-

---

1 Interview with Farzam, September 2013.

tremely upset. I understand that the government wants to reduce the number of exempted individuals but they must have found a different way. This policy is not fair and does not take into account the situation of transsexuals who are rejected by their families, have no job and money, and cannot simply afford to undergo sex reassignment surgery within a six-month period.[1]

A number of reported cases suggest that as a result of the new regulation, gay and transgender individuals are being contacted within several months of receiving the temporary exemption, and asked to submit themselves to hormone therapy and sex reassignment procedures. This was the case of Ashkan, a twenty-year-old gay man from Kermanshah, who is now an asylum seeker in Turkey:

> I did a lot of research to find out if one can apply for exemption based on homosexuality, and also whether it is a dangerous method or not. So I went to visit a psychologist I had known for years who knew me very well. He advised that I go to a psychiatrist that specializes in neurology, and referred me to one. This psychiatrist asked for an extended therapy period – so I visited him for three months – after which he was sure that he could write a letter to the Military Service Office that would get me started on the exemption process. The letter I got from him indicated his diagnosis as "Gender Identity Disorder." And this was the worst thing he could have diagnosed me with, because it could have changed my fate: I did not know that this diagnosis did not imply homosexuality, and I did not bother to research it and find out more about it.

1 Interview with Mohammad, October 2013.

I took this letter to the exemption office...and received an exemption based on it. After this, I was obviously very happy. I was going to get my passport to emigrate from Iran, and I was merely waiting for my partner to finish his studies so we could leave together. But a different fate was awaiting us. Three months after receiving the exemption, a letter arrived which demanded that I introduce myself by a certain date to Dr. Mir Jalaali at a specific location in Tehran and begin my hormone therapy. I would then have to take my hormone therapy results to the Medical Commission of the Military Service to renew my exemption. I had been exempted for a six-month period only. Also, by a certain date, I had to visit a court to receive an order from a judge for a sex reassignment operation.

When I told my mother about this, she could only scream and cry. A friend of mine told me that it was a terrible idea to go there and introduce myself as a homosexual to the judge: "he is not a doctor who may assume that your homosexuality is a sickness that can be cured. He is a judge, and he can sentence you based on your own confession. This is extremely dangerous." But what was I to do? I could not have gone through with the sex reassignment operation and ruin my own life. I did not want to change my gender; I was happy with the person I was. Perhaps when I turn thirty, I will not even wear make-up anymore and will dress like an ordinary man. I had the right to stay a man: I did not want to be a woman, and I did not want to lose my partner. I did not want to lose my family. If I went through with the operation, I would lose everything: I would be kicked out on the streets, and my mother and everybody else would never accept me again. I would have to build my life from scratch. So I could not stay in

Iran anymore: I left, and my boyfriend, who did not have a passport, left illegally afterwards. [1]

As with the process of legal gender recognition, the process of obtaining an exemption from military service is replete with instances of abuse against gay and transgender individuals. A number of interviewees told JFI & 6Rang that they were required to undress in front of the Medical Commission of the Military Service in order to obtain an exemption. Faraz, a female-to-male transsexual said:

> The officer responsible for processing my exemption request was unable to comprehend my situation. He did not understand why I had had testicular implant surgery, and he did not know anything about transsexuality. He just kept insisting that he must see my genitals. I was really getting hurt at that moment. He asked me to pull down my pants behind this small curtain, and meanwhile all these people were passing by, wanting to peek inside and see what was happening. I would try to cover myself with my hands, but he kept shoving my hands aside. In the end, he managed to see my genitals and asked: "where's your thing? You have your balls, but no penis." He wrote in my letter: "absence of penis." My friend had been through this process before and I knew through him that I needed to object to his assessment. I told him I need this exemption to leave the country and receive my phalloplasty operation and it was problematic for him to identify my condition as "lack of penis" because I was going to have one upon my return. I told him that he should have written "bigender" instead…

This was unfortunately not the end of the process. In order to verify my file, I had to attend a session be-

---

1 Interview with Ashkan, January 2013.

fore the Medical Commission of the Military Service, which consisted of one doctor, and three military officers…Just picture yourself in a room where people with various medical problems have sat in different places and ten of them have lined up behind a small curtain, waiting for their turns to come. In this midst of all these, you are asked to go behind a curtain and pull your pants down. You have no idea what a terrible experience this was. The doctor played with my testicles with his pen while saying: "that's it?" And mind you he could be considered a nice guy because he did not at least stare at it for far too long. After he finished his "examination," one of the officers came forward and said that he must see it too. I asked the officer "why do you have to see it?" and he said: "just joking." I was quite angry at that point and responded: "I'm not on joking terms with you." Those moments were very bad and difficult moments.[1]

Kaveh, another female-to-male transsexual who was also forced to undress, told JFI & 6Rang how the Medical Commission of the Military Service subjected him to an unprofessional examination with unwanted touching, verbal harassment and "involuntary outing":

I visited the military service office of the city of Karaj and they told me that I needed to go to a certain office in Tehran to be physically examined. The responsible examiner at that office was apparently a doctor. "Pull down your pants" he said. I asked: "what is it that you want to see?" He said that he had to see my genitals before he could confirm that I was a transsexual. Standing at a distance, I pulled down my underwear and said: "here, see it." He came near and touched my vagina. I hated my genitals so much that I never touched them myself and now there was

---

1 Interview with Faraz, January 2013.

this guy, touching my vagina without my consent. I said: "what are you doing?" He answered: "I have to see what it is." I said: "it is nothing special, haven't you ever seen one in your life?" It was close to turning into a brawl...I was trembling. Eventually, he gave me a document, which I needed to take back to the military service office in Karaj.

Later, over at the Karaj office, I had another terrible experience: only men visit this office and there were so many of them – nearly two hundred... No one but me was a transsexual. We were all lined against a wall, and each time they would call 25 applicants to visit the small office upstairs. The authorities in charge would loudly call people out with their names and health problems and inform them of the type of exemption they were going to receive.

I had already waited three hours for my turn, and meanwhile one of the applicants in the line had been questioning me about my health problem. I had to lie to him, and said that I had a heart problem. He was there with me in that tiny office when my turn finally arrived. The officer pronounced my problem out loud: "identity disorder." This officer was an idiot and had difficulty pronouncing the word "transsexual." The officer sitting next to him was a bit better. He corrected his pronunciation. The first officer asked, "What does it mean?" and the second one yelled out, "it means he used to be a woman but he is now a man." All of the sudden the entire room burst into chatter, curious about my situation. I was too embarrassed to raise my head at that moment. The first officer said, "What? I don't get it." The other officer, who apparently had encountered a similar case before, said, "They have identity disorders." The first officer turned to me and asked, "So you yourself chose to become a man? You didn't have a sexual disorder?" And when I asked them to speak quietly, he said: "if you have a problem with it, then get out of here." I had no choice but to cope with the situation because I was leaving for Istanbul in one month's time and I needed to get my exemption certificate as quickly as possible. The first officer asked: "Well, then what? Did you ask for the surgery?" I answered: "yes, it's a psychological disorder. I had no control over this. I was like this since I was very young." He shook his head, indicating that he did not understand, and added: "so how do we make sure that you are in fact a transsexual?" I said: "So when a person with a heart problem comes to you, do you find out on your own that he has a problem? He has been to a doctor to conform this, and you sent me to a doctor too." There was a curtained partition in the room. He asked me to go in there and pull down my pants. I said: "why should I do this in front of all these people? Everyone can see me"...But I had no choice. I ended up pulling down my pants and he said: "You have done nothing there. It's still what it was [i.e. a vagina]. Why have you come here asking for exemption? There's no reason for you go to military at all."

People were chattering and I was trembling. I had no self-confidence left and could do nothing to change the situation. Finally the other officer said: "they have identity disorders. We must give them permanent exemption. Only at war time they have to serve." I felt so belittled as I was leaving the room. Everybody was staring at me. When my mother asked why I looked so miserable and disheveled, I said: "it's nothing. Throughout all these years I had never been crushed like this." She kept urging me to be strong, but I had reached my limit. Why did I have to go through surgery and all those other diffi-

culties if I still had to pull down my pants every-
where I went? In those days, my beard had grown
and my voice had become more masculine. But my
identification documents had not changed. So I was
still referred to as "miss." This made people stare at
me and wonder whether I was a boy or girl. [1]

Farzam, another female-to-male transsexual, had a similar experience with a physician of the Revolutionary Guards in Tehran:

The officer asked for my file and said: "what is your
medical problem?" I could not bring myself to say it
out loud given all the people who were standing
around. So I put down my finger on the word 'sex
reassignment.' He said: "what is your problem?" I
said, here, look. He did not try to understand me. He
yelled at me: "I said what is your problem? Why are
you pointing at this?" The more I tried to show him
the word, the angrier he got and yelled louder. But all
of a sudden he saw what I was pointing at, and yelled
out: "Doctor, it's a sex reassignment case... You go
in that room and pull down your pants." Embarrassed, I headed for the room, and by the time the
doctor got to see me, I was feeling utterly horrified
about the prospect of being examined by him. I had
undergone surgery only recently and did not have a
penis yet. I stood on my feet, and the doctor kneeled
down to examine me and asked a set of fairly personal questions...He was unfamiliar with the topic
but he was a young doctor and his manners were not
unpleasant...The behavior of the person who was
standing behind the desk was, however, quite terrible... He must have understood that I was feeling

1 Interview with Kaveh, January 2013.

uncomfortable and there was no reason for him to announce my condition out loud.[1]

As the preceding discussion demonstrates, the process of legal gender recognition in Iran consists of three main elements or phases: namely, psychiatric diagnosis, hormone therapy and surgery to change the genitalia and other secondary sexual characteristics. Transgender individuals are forced to go through all three phases in order to obtain legal gender recognition and enjoy their fundamental human rights. This is while the Standards of Care has made clear that the diagnosis of Gender Dysphoria "invites the consideration of a variety of therapeutic options, only one of which is the complete therapeutic triad."[2]

In 1992, the European Court of Human Rights first recognized that a state's refusal to allow transgender people to change the gender markers on their official documents was a violation of the European Convention on Human Rights.[3] In 2006, the Yogyakarta Principles, which crystallize the current status of human rights law in relation to gender identity and sexual orientation, stipulated that: "No person may be forced to undergo any form of medical or psychological treatment, procedure, testing, or be confined to a medical facility, based on sexual orientation or gender identity. Notwithstanding any classifications to the contrary, a person's sexual orientation and gender identity are not, in and of themselves, medical conditions and are not to be treated, cured or suppressed."[4] In 2013, the UN Special Rapporteur on Torture raised concern about practices that require transgender persons "to un-

---

1 Interview with Farzam, September 2013.

2 World Professional Association for Transgender Health, "Standards of Care for Gender Identity Disorders," Sixth Version (2001), p. 3, online: http://www.wpath.org/documents2/socv6.pdf (Retrieved on 4 May 2014).

3 European Court of Human Rights, *B. v France*, no. 13343/87 (1992).

4 Yogyakarta Principles on the application of international human rights law in relation to sexual orientation and gender identity, online: http://www.yogyakartaprinciples.org/principles_en.htm (Retrieved on 15 January 2014).

dergo often unwanted sterilization surgeries as a prerequisite to enjoy legal recognition of their preferred gender" and called upon states to put an end to these practices.[1]

Despite these developments, Iran continues to make the change in one's legal gender contingent on the fulfillment of invasive medical treatments through abusive and degrading procedures. This violates the right of transgender people to be free from inhuman, cruel or degrading treatment, which is protected under several international human rights instruments including the ICCPR (Article 7) and the UN Convention against Torture and Inhuman, Cruel or Degrading Treatment or Punishment (Article 16). It also impairs and nullifies the equal enjoyment by transgender people of their rights to liberty and personal security, privacy, education, work, and the highest attainable standard of health.

---

1 Report of the Special Rapporteur on torture and other cruel, inhuman or degrading treatment or punishment, Juan E. Mendez, A/HRC/22/53 (1 February 2013), at para.78.

5. Torment in the Name of Treatment: Abuses Against Lesbian, Gay and Transgender Persons in Health-Care Settings

In an interview with Channel 2 of the Islamic Republic of Iran Broadcasting in March 2013, Mohamamd Javad Ardeshir Larijani, the head of Iran's Human Rights Commission said:

> Homosexuality is an illness, a very bad illness. Therefore, organizing gatherings and publicizing the issue, and so on is an offence. We have strict laws in this regard and we respond rigorously. As for the treatment of individuals however, we do not think it is right to beat and bully [homosexuals]. They are sick people who must be treated. They have to be put under psychiatric care and sometime even biological and physical care. We need to adopt a clinical and medical approach toward this issue. But the West intends to introduce it [homosexuality] as a normal social behavior and we are completely against this notion.[1]

This chapter documents some of the psychiatric and physical treatments that lesbian, gay and transgender people have been subjected to, as per Mr. Larijani's recommendation, in order to be cured of their homosexuality.

Focusing on the theme of medical abuses committed on the basis of homosexual orientation and transgender identity, the chapter also documents the pain and suffering experienced by transgender and transsexual people as a result of negligent sex reassignment procedures that have been administered without

---

1 See https://www.youtube.com/watch?v=8Wh0snjDCX0 (Retrieved on 18 June 2014).

informed consent, and in reckless disregard of international standards of care for the health of transsexual and transgender people. In both instances, the chapter demonstrates how institutions involved in the delivery of health-care in Iran interfere with the human dignity and personal integrity of lesbian, gay and transgender people, stigmatizing their identities, wounding their bodies and diminishing their mental and physical health as well as emotional and social well-being.

Abuses addressed in this chapter lead to international responsibility for the Iranian State, regardless of whether they are perpetrated by state-affiliated or private physicians, as they are being committed with the consent and acquiescence of state officials, who admittedly show a total disregard for Iran's international obligation to protect lesbian, gay and transgender people against cruel, inhuman or degrading treatment and other human rights violations, including those committed by medical professionals.

5.1. Background & Context

Lesbian, gay and transgender individuals in Iran may suffer social isolation, distorted self-image and emotional anguish as a result of being stigmatized and criminalized for their expressions of gender variance and same-sex attraction. In a society where rigid boundaries are drawn between men and women, and discriminatory rules such as mandatory veiling and sex segregation are enforced, the preference of lesbian, gay and transgender individuals for behaviors usually associated with the gender other than the one they were assigned at birth, may often create such anxiety for their parents that they are pressured to consult mental health professionals. Finding themselves stigmatized and isolated from family and friends, they may also self-present to medical authorities in order to discuss the uncertainty and emotional distress that they experience regarding their gender identification and sexual orientation.

To their dismay and disappointment however, lesbian, gay and transgender people frequently find that health-care professionals lack knowledge regarding issues relating to sexual orientation and gender identity. The experience of Saba is reflective of this lack of knowledge and training:

> I never found the courage to visit a psychiatrist. So I studied psychology on my own to better understand my situation. Once, in a psychological text, I read that a combination of hormonal malfunctions may lead to the desire for the same sex, so I paid a visit to an endocrinologist to test my hormones…I told him about my desire for the same sex, and asked him to submit me to a complete blood test that checks for adrenal gland secretions and sexual hormones. He got quite surprised but submitted me for the test anyway…The city I lived in was very religious and the clinic I visited was located in a particularly religious neighborhood in which one could only get around by wearing a chador [an outer garment or open cloak worn by some Iranian women in public spaces]. So imagine a young woman wearing a chador entering a male doctor's office, sitting down in front of him, and asking him to write her a blood test because she has same-sex sexual desires…I did the test and because I knew of the factors that I needed to look for in my results, I did not visit him again. I read the results myself and they indicated normal levels of hormone. During the visitation, the doctor also asked me several questions that were primarily of a medical nature. He weighed me and said: "your weight is very low; gaining some weight will resolve your problem." He even gave me some weight-gain supplements, emphasizing that my problem was due to my slenderness. In other words, he believed that my sexual desires were caused by my weight. I am not sure what his medical reasons were. Perhaps he thought

that my body was thin and had not sexually matured enough to secrete sexual hormones.[1]

Lack of knowledge on the part of medical professionals is frequently accompanied by a bias against any form of gender or sexual identification that challenges heteronormative social stereotypes. This bias manifests itself in the use of pejorative and condemnatory terms which have caused or exacerbated distress and poor mental health in lesbian, gay and transgender individuals. Soheil told JFI & 6Rang:

> More often than not, psychiatrists have caused me trouble. My mother and I once visited a renowned psychiatrist who claimed to have got his doctorate from England. He told my mother that I am a pervert. He used the exact same term. He said, "Your daughter is a sexual pervert; leave her be, so she full around. We have a similar person in our family who spends money on women, goes around, and one can do nothing about it other than waiting for her to hit rock bottom and change." I found these comments extremely offensive. I had gone to the doctor looking for a solution, and he was instead degrading me. He was basically saying that I am sexually deviant and my mother should not bother with me. As a result of his comments, my mother grew more sensitive toward me and her entire demeanor began to change to the point that my friends could not come over to our house anymore. I felt so down, both emotionally and psychologically, that I developed schizophrenic tendencies. I felt my soul did not belong to my body and worms were eating me from inside. I felt like I was decomposing. If a person pulled hard on my arm, I would ask him to let go of it, because I thought worms were gnawing at it. I was schizophrenic for six months, and during this period I had

1 Interview with Saba, August 2012.

a lot of problems with my family. The situation had got so bad that my mother would sit on the prayer mat, lift her hands in prayer to God, cry tears and wish for me to get run over by a truck and never return home again. I used to think my mother's wish was bound to come true.[1]

Nima, another female-to-male transsexual, shared a similar experience of verbal abuse. When he was thirty-one years old and still a female legally, he went to a gynecology clinic in search of professional advice:

I did not really know what kind of doctor I needed to visit but I chose a women's specialist. The doctor stared at me in disbelief when I described myself for her and her gaze was enough to make me feel embarrassed for who I was. She had me lying down on the examination table and inspected me from behind her magnifying glass while saying some stuff about potential abnormalities with my ovaries, which I utterly failed to understand. She then submitted me for an ultrasonography test. I did the test and visited her again. After seeing the results, she said that my uterus and ovaries were normal and I did not have a biological problem. She then said that there is nothing wrong with having sex with women and that she could refer to me a place where I could get a dildo. I was absolutely dumbfounded by her attitude. She was treating me as though I had a penis complex… During the examination, she offered to surgically remove my hymen. When I asked why, she said: "so your girlfriend can stick in a dildo for you." This comment enraged me and I began to yell at her…I left the hefty fee she charged me on her desk, and slammed the door behind me. While leaving, she called me by my first name and said, "once you learn

1 Interview with Soheil, July 2012.

more about your condition, come down and explain it to me too." This negative experience distressed me a lot.[1]

The findings of this research suggest that many Iranian mental health professionals still believe that homosexuality is a form of mental illness, and gender variance is in and of itself a pathological condition. Accordingly, instead of supporting their clients in identity exploration and development without pursuing predetermined outcomes, they have come to pre-scribe treatments that mainly revolve around converting ho-mosexual orientation and aligning sex, gender and sexuality. Broadly speaking, these treatments for changing sexual arousal patterns and modifying gender expressions fall into one of the two following models:

The first model advocates a range of psychoanalytical and be-havioral treatments that are focused on creating a qualitative mental change involving aversion to homosexuality, and disat-tachment to trans-dressing and other gender variant tenden-cies. In practice, these treatments tend to be accompanied by a reinforcement plan in which shaming techniques, nausea-inducing and psychoactive medications, and electroshocks are used. Mental health professionals in Iran who follow this model insist on the efficacy and benefit of such sexual orien-tation and gender identity change efforts even though these practices have been internationally denounced as unscientific, harmful and a violation of human rights.[2]

---

1 Interview with Nima, August 2012.

2 An example of this approach is found in a scholarly project published in the LMOI quarterly reports, in which three psychiatrists explain a reparative method based on long-term psychiatric medication which they allegedly successfully tested on four individuals who presented physical or behavioral characteristics associated with the gender other than the one assigned at birth and expressed desire for the same sex: Dr. Alireza Zahi-roddin et al, "ravan darman-I movaffaghiat amiz-i chihar mored-i ikhtelal-i hoviat-i jensi [Effective Psychotherapeutic Treatment of Four Cases of Gender Identity Disorder]" (Spring 2005) 37 *Majaley-i Elmi-I Pezeshky-i Qanuni Scientific* 37 [The Scientific Journal of the Legal Medicine Organization], online:
http://www.sid.ir/fa/VEWSSID/J_pdf/60613843707.pdf (Retrieved on 4 May 2014).

The second model concedes that treatments aimed at converting one's experienced sexual orientation and gender identity are generally without success, and advocates instead that the body of transgender people be altered and brought into conformity with their psyche through hormone therapy and sex reassignment surgeries. Mental health professionals who follow this model are generally inclined to assign a diagnosis of Gender Identity Disorder to lesbian, gay and transgender persons, and to take social gender non-conformity, homosexual orientation, and consequences of social prejudice and stigma (such as depression, isolation, confusion and distorted self-image) as symptomatic of this disorder. This has rendered lesbian, gay and transgender persons susceptible to being misdiagnosed as having a "Gender Identity Disorder," and rushed into irreversible hormone therapy and sex reassignment surgeries. They are rarely provided with a meaningful opportunity to explore their same-sex desires and gender expressions, and access accurate information on issues related to sexual orientation and gender identity.

The foregoing medical models share a presumption of inherent mental illness for homosexuality and gender variance, and understand a healthy gender identity as one that is dimorphic, singular and heterosexual.[1] This is while internationally accepted manuals such as the fourth and fifth editions of the DSM have increasingly tried to move away from binary understandings of gender and defined the goal of psychotherapeutic, endocrinal or surgical therapy as one of facilitating

---

1 This view is generally endorsed by mental health professionals and scholarship. Dr. Behnam Ohadi who has extensively written in support of the theory that physical differences have been observed in certain anatomical structures of the brain, such as the pituitary gland, of homosexual individuals compared to "normal" individuals, writes: "A number physical differences have been observed in certain anatomical structures of the brain in individuals with Gender Identity Disorder compared to normal individuals. This could be due to abnormal transformations of the anatomic structure of the brain during early developments of the Central Nervous System of the embryo which were not consistent and in line with the patient's natural gender." Behnam Ohadi et al, "Brain Imaging Characteristics of the Brain in Patients with Gender Identity Disorder and Normal Individuals" (Fall 2007) 9(3) *Advancements in Cognitive Science* 20, online: http://sid.ir/Fa/VEWSSID/J_pdf/68113863508.pdf (Retrieved on 4 May 2014).

lasting personal comfortable with one's sexual and gendered self rather than eradicating gender variant expressions.

Questions that Rayan was asked at her first consultation with a psychotherapist, whom her parents pressured her to meet, shows how much the discourse and practice of mental health-care professionals in Iran lags behind these international developments:

> In my high school years, one of those counselors who really don't understand anything told me such ridiculous things that years later, when I recounted them during my UN interview, my lawyer could not but burst into laughter. One day I noticed my parents secretly murmuring in the kitchen. Then my mother came out and asked me to accompany her somewhere. When I asked where, she spoke of this counselor I had to visit. I told her that I wouldn't go, that I was tired of being treated as though I am sick. She began yelling and shouting in response and I left for my room. I had an intimate emotional relationship with my father, so he tried to console me afterwards. He said that I should not refuse ... as that would only make matters worse, and suggested that we continue the discussion at the counselor's office. I told my father that I would go only if he accompanied us to the counselor's office. So I ended up going, along with my father and mother.

> At the office, the first question the counselor asked me was: "How are you?" I said: "Very well, thank you." He was going to analyze my responses to find out whether I was a lesbian or not, and I guess this was his way of starting the process. He then said: "I have a question: in your dreams, when you're walking on the clouds, are you holding a woman's hands, or a man's?" I stared at him in disbelief. My plan then was to lie because my family still knew nothing about

my sexual orientation and was simply suspicious. I
told him: "Of course a man's!" He then asked me
another stupid question: "Why don't you wear high
heels?" I said: "It bothers my feet, doctor, and
frankly it hurts my back when I walk. But other than
that, I have no problem with wearing high heels." He
said, "Why don't you wear make-up?" and I said,
"My skin feels itchy when I wear make make-up, and
lipstick makes my lips greasy, which disgusts me."
After this, he asked me to leave the room and called
my mother in...Back at home, my mother said: "you
could deceive the doctor but you will never be able
to deceive me." When I asked why she was saying
this, she said: "The counselor said your daughter
does not have any problem, and she's even more
normal than normal girls." I told her: "A counselor
who begins the conversation with such questions
can't truly be a counselor." My mother had found his
contact information in one of those rubbish maga-
zines thrown at every doorstep.[1]

Rayan believes that she had a high chance of being perceived
as a transsexual if she were to speak the truth about her same-
sex attractions and lack of interest in feminine presentation.
Experiences of lesbian women like Sarah and Elnaz confirm
this suspicion. Sarah told JFI & 6Rang:

I was about twenty-two years old when I informed
my family of my homosexual orientation. My sister
knew about it from two years back, but my mother
and father did not know. When I told my mother,
she readily accepted it, which was rather surprising to
me... I asked my mother to speak to my father about
it. My father was very religious but he did not react
inappropriately either and only insisted that I see a
counselor – which I did for a couple of sessions...

---

1 Interview with Rayan, August 2012.

The sessions did not get anywhere, leading the counselor to finally say that there is no use in continuing
"because I was not willing to alter my preferences."..
When visiting the counselor, my sister used to come
along and interfere with the counseling process.
Once, she brought in pictures from our childhood
when she was dressed very "girly," and I, very "boy-
ish." I liked dressing that way throughout my childhood. By showing these pictures, she was trying to
point out what was according to her my masculine
traits, even though in my opinion the choice of attire
is simply a construct and not inherent to being man
or woman. This and other things ultimately led the
therapist to perceive me as being a transsexual... In
our sessions together, he did not use the word transsexual, but pressed that I have the traits and characteristics of a man. He insisted on this opinion despite
my repeated attempts to refute it. He said the same
thing to my dad. After that, my dad brought up the
issue of sex change and to this day he continues to
persist with the belief that I want to be a man.[1]

Elnaz had a similar counseling experience. In her early twen-
ties, she was misdiagnosed with transsexualism because she
did not conform to society's notions of how a woman should
dress and act:

My psychiatrist, Dr. Mojtahed Zaadeh, asked me a
couple of quick questions relating to my appearance
such as: "Do you like wearing make-up, or nail pol-
ish? Do you like wearing women's clothing?" I answered "no," and this led him to conclude that I was
transsexual. I also told him about the intimate relationship I had with my mother, and my poor relationship with my father; how, not only from an emotional standpoint but also physically I was more com-

---

1 Interview with Sarah, April 2013.

fortable with my mother, which was the opposite of how my female friends preferred physical contact with their fathers... The psychiatrist found this to be of paramount importance. Having diagnosed me with Gender Identity Disorder, he referred me to the "Prevention Office" of the State Welfare Organization...I went there with one of my female friends and when they saw us together, they immediately thought we are partners and referred me to one of their caseworkers. They told me that I had to talk to a social worker before submitting an application for sex reassignment to the court. I did not go to the social worker, and instead went to Dr. Mir Jalaali, which was a huge mistake. One does not resort to Dr. Mir Jalaali immediately, because he is only too eager to operate. He received me cordially, listened to my words carefully, and then agreed to perform my operation. He told me only one thing and it was that "I cannot second guess the operation as there's no coming back from it" and that "I must have thoroughly thought this over." At that point, I said that I didn't have a problem with it.[1]

Elnaz was later dissuaded from pursuing sex reassignment procedures. She sought the opinion of two other psychiatrists and both diagnosed her condition as being "lesbianism" and not "transsexualism."

The majority of those interviewed for this research were identified by their psychiatrists or counselors as being transsexual within one or two sessions, and subsequently advised to pursue sex reassignment procedures. This is how Kaveh, a twenty-six-year-old female-to-male transsexual, related his experience:

---

1 Interview with Elnaz, September 2012.

> My psychiatrist was a young man. I visited him a couple of times. During these two sessions, he asked about my sexual interests and fantasies, and concluded on that basis that I was a transsexual and had to undergo surgery. I told him that I had no idea how to tell this to my parents. I was only eighteen at the time and very naïve – and nothing like today's eighteen year olds. I was into sports and soccer, and had never been sexually involved with anyone. During these two sessions we spoke for two hours, and in the end he said: "you are transsexual and you must undergo [sex reassignment] surgery."[1]

Sepehr had a similar experience. He identifies as a gay man who sometimes wears makeup and what is considered stereotypically "feminine" clothing. At his first consultation, he was told that he is a transsexual on the basis of his gender expressions and same-sex attractions:

> The first time I visited a psychiatrist and told him about being in love with a boy, he simply asked me to "try dating girls." I told him that I had tried with women but I was still in love with that boy. He said: "well, do you want to change your sex?" I was shocked. I responded: "No, I'm fine. Why should I change my sex?" My friends have had the same experience. I think psychiatrists in Iran are truly responsible for recirculating fascistic attitudes toward homosexuality...They pathologize you...and want to either electroshock you into being straight or remove your testicles. This is a very prevalent attitude, and I experienced it with three different psychiatrists, and so did my friends. We actually do not know of a sin-

---

1 Interview with Kaveh, January 2013.

gle psychiatrist who is equipped with a decent knowledge of homosexuality.[1]

The foregoing diagnostic practices stand in stark contrast to international standards, including the UN Principles for the Protection of Persons with Mental Illness and for the Improvement for Mental Health Care, which states in Principle 4 that "[a] determination of mental illness shall never be made on the basis of political…or social status, or membership in a cultural … or religious group, or for any other reason not directly relevant to mental health status," and "non-conformity with moral, social, cultural or political values or religious beliefs prevailing in a person's community, shall never be a determining factor in the diagnosis of mental illness." [2]

5.2. Reparative Therapies

Reparative therapies, also called aversion, conversion or reorientation therapies, generally refer to attempts to change sexual orientation and "cure" individuals of homosexuality, cross-gender behavior, or gender non-conformity at large, based on pathological conceptions of the foregoing. They include a wide range of pseudo-medical interventions, such as forced psychiatric interventions,[3] hormone therapy, unnecessary and non-consensual medication, use of electroshock or electroconvulsive therapy (ECT),[4] as well as a variety of forced pro-

---

1 Interview with Sepehr, March 2013.

2 United Nations General Assembly Resolution No A/RES/46/119, A/46/PV.75 (17 December 1991), principle 4.

3 A comprehensive account on the use of psychiatry as a means of torture or ill-treatment in the context of aversion therapies inflicted in order to attempt to suppress, control and modify the sexual orientation of individuals by a number of states has been documented by Amnesty International in "*Crimes of hate, conspiracy of silence torture and ill-treatment based on sexual identity*" AI index ACT 40/016/2007 (2000).

4 As the Special Rapporteur reported in 2008, unmodified electroshock therapy may inflict severe pain and suffering and often leads to medical consequences, including bone, ligament and spinal fractures, cognitive deficits and possible loss of memory. It cannot be considered as an acceptable medical practice and may constitute torture or ill-treatment. →

cedures such as sterilization and genital-normalizing surgeries imposed on persons with atypical sex characteristics [intersex persons], often involving humiliation, psychiatric misdiagnosis and wrongful determination of mental illness.

Aside from the physical abuse often associated with such practices, many of these have been found to have serious negative repercussions on the mental and psychological health of the individuals undergoing such therapies. The American Psychoanalytic Association (APA) 1999 position statement on reparative therapy states that "[p]sychoanalytic technique does not encompass purposeful attempts to "convert," "repair," change or shift an individual's sexual orientation, gender identity or gender expression. Such directed efforts are against fundamental principles of psychoanalytic treatment and often result in substantial psychological pain by reinforcing damaging internalized attitudes."[1] In an earlier Resolution on Appropriate Therapeutic Responses to Sexual Orientation, APA reaffirmed its opposition to "portrayals of lesbian, gay, and bisexual youths and adults as mentally ill due to their sexual orientation" and defined appropriate interventions as those that "counteract bias that is based on ignorance or unfounded beliefs about sexual orientation."[2]

In a position statement issued on May 17 2012, the Pan American Health Organization, the North and South American branch of the World Health Organization, renewed its call

---

← In its modified form, it is of vital importance that electroshock therapy be administered only with the free and informed consent of the person concerned, including on the basis of information on the secondary effects and related risks such as heart complications, confusion, loss of memory and even death. See Interim report of the Special Rapporteur on torture and other cruel, inhuman or degrading treatment or punishment, A/63/175 (28 July 2008), para 61.

1 American Psychiatric Association, *Attempts to Change Sexual Orientation, Gender Identity, or Gender Expression: Position statement* (1999) (now replaced by a position statement under the same title, 2012), online:
http://www.apsa.org/About_APsaA/Position_Statements/Attempts_to_Change_Sexual_Orientation.aspx (Retrieved on May 3, 2014)

2 American Psychological Association, *Resolution on appropriate therapeutic responses to sexual orientation, American Psychologist* (1998), pp. 934-935.

for caution against services that purport to "cure" people with non-heterosexual sexual orientations as they lack medical justification and represent a serious threat to the health and well-being of affected people. The statement noted the global scientific and professional consensus on the fact that homosexuality is a normal and natural variation of human sexuality and cannot be regarded as a pathological condition.[1] The WPATH has similarly considered that treatments specifically aimed at trying to change a person's gender expression to become more congruent with the sex assigned at birth are generally unsuccessful and can no longer be considered ethical.[2]

Of equal importance to the topic of reparative therapies is Principle 9 of the UN Principles for the Protection of Persons with Mental Illness and for the Improvement for Mental Health Care, which requires that mental health treatment "always be provided in accordance with applicable standards of ethics for mental health practitioners, including internationally accepted standards" and "be directed towards preserving and enhancing personal autonomy."[3] Principle 10 of the same resolution requires that medication "meet the best health needs of the patient" and "be given to a patient only for therapeutic or diagnostic purposes." To this end, the resolution forbids administration of medication as "a punishment or for the convenience of others" and obliges mental health

1 Therapies to Change Sexual Orientation Lack Medical Justification and Threaten Health" (PAHO/WHO, 2012), online:
http://www.paho.org/hq/index.php?option=com_content&view=article&id=6803%3A%5C%22therapies%5C%22-to-change-sexual-orientation-lack-medical-justification-and-threaten-health-&catid=740%3Anews-press-releases&Itemid=1926&lang=en (Retrieved on May 3, 2014).

2 World Professional Association for Transgender Health, "Standards of Care for the Health of Transsexual, Transgender and Gender Non Conforming People," Seventh Version (2012), p. 32, online:
http://www.wpath.org/uploaded_files/140/files/Standards%20of%20Care,%20V7%20Full%20Book.pdf (Retrieved on 4 May 2014).

3 United Nations General Assembly Resolution No A/RES/46/119, A/46/PV.75, 17 December 1991, principle 9.

practitioners to "only administer medication of known or demonstrated efficacy."[1]

Drawing from the foregoing principles and positions, the Special Rapporteur on Torture has condemned the use of reparative therapies, noting that "[t]hese procedures are rarely medically necessary, can cause scarring, loss of sexual sensation, pain, incontinence and lifelong depression and have also been criticized as being unscientific, potentially harmful and contributing to stigma."[2]

The accounts of lesbian, gay and transgender individuals interviewed for this report show, however, that the majority of mental health professionals in Iran have total disregard for the foregoing international developments, and still hold false or deceptive opinions regarding the scientific basis of sexual orientation and gender identity change efforts.

A troubling number of lesbian, gay and transgender individuals with whom JFI & 6Rang spoke reported that their psychiatrists prescribed strong psychoactive medications such as thioridazine, citalopram, fluoxetine, risperidone, and bipyridine, in order to control or modify their sexual arousal patterns, even though such medication are best reserved for serious mental illnesses. Mehrad, a seventeen-year-old female-to-male transsexual, was given psychoactive medications when he was fifteen years old in order to eliminate "his homosexual tendencies":

> My father's spouse recommended that we pay a visit to a psychiatrist. In the city of Shahroud there was a young psychiatrist renowned for his work. I visited him and talked to him about my characteristics and behaviors. He said: "You are not transsexual. Rather,

1 United Nations General Assembly Resolution No A/RES/46/119, A/46/PV.75, 17 December 1991, principle 10.

2 Report of the Special Rapporteur on torture and other cruel, inhuman or degrading treatment or punishment, Juan E. Méndez, A/HRC/22/53, 1 February 2013, at para 76.

you have homosexual tendencies." I expressed my doubts but he insisted on his opinion and right there prescribed a combination of drugs that he said would fix me.[1]

Nima, another female-to-male transsexual, had a similar experience when he was thirty-two years old:

> I asked my doctor if there was a way I could change my sex in response to which she said: "you have got a mental problem; visit a psychiatrist to take care of it. He will give you sleeping pills and this and that medication and that will resolve your issues." She then gave me some anti-depressants to take home. I slipped into depression within a month of using them.[2]

Kia is another female-to-male transsexual who was prescribed large doses of psychoactive medication because of his homosexual desires. He shared with JFI & 6Rang the repercussions of such unjustified medication:

> I was a happy, healthy seventeen-year-old who did sports and did not suffer from any severe depression. I just had a [Gender Identity] disorder. The pills that I was given are normally prescribed to people with severe mental conditions who must be hospitalized. I was given such pills just because I had expressed a sense of dissatisfaction with my situation. The pills turned out to be a heavy substance for a teenage body that had never consumed any narcotics or alcohol. They numbed my entire body... to the point that I had become incontinent. I burst into tears when I found myself to be wet in the morning. I felt like I had been raped. The notion of rape should not

---

1 Interview with Mehrad, August 2012.

2 Interview with Nima, August 2012.

be understood only in relation to sexual relations; I really felt as if this doctor had raped and violated me. This experience made me lose trust in all doctors.[1]

In addition to harmful medication, some interviewees were submitted to electroshock therapy in order to be cured of their homosexuality. Polina, a twenty-three year-old lesbian woman, told JFI & 6Rang that she was given medication and electroshocks at the age of fourteen after her parents took her to a psychiatrist in Tehran for her anger, anxiety, depression and suicidal ideation, which they believed was caused by her sexual orientation. In her interview with JFI & 6Rang, Polina explained that her distress was linked to isolation, stigma, shame, and her deteriorated relationships with her mother, who controlled her movements, prevented her from developing friendships with other girls, and subjected her to hostile remarks, but her doctor did not provide her with any resources to aid her self-awareness and self-acceptance amid this social context of stigma and parental rejection, and instead gave her prescription drugs to change her sexual orientation:

> Dr. Bandshahi did not usually talk to me in our sessions with each other. He would often only listen and take notes of what I said and then hand me a prescription. When he said anything, his main talking point was that "ok you want to be friends with a girl, go ahead and do that but it is not necessary that you tell this to your mom. He asked me why I continue with this behavior and why I insist on talking to my girlfriend on the phone when my mom is at home. But I did this because I wanted the tension to be resolved and that my parents accept who I am.

> In that period, I cried day and night. I did not study and could not do much. I had grown so tired of the

1 Interview with Kia, October 2013.

tensions and conflicts at home that I accepted to take all the drugs that Dr. Bandshahi had prescribed me. The drugs caused weight gain and made my whole body to swell. I slept all night and most of the day and did not understand life anymore. My mother constantly teased and taunted me about how this straight girl whom I was friends with had left me and how these kinds of affairs never continue. Getting bombarded with these comments over and over, I started to feel that there is no point at all in living my life if I am not attracted to men and I always risk being abandoned by women I come to love. I felt disgusted with myself.

JFI & 6Rang understands that when Polina shared her negative emotions of self-hatred and suicidality with her doctor, her doctor expressed disappointment that despite one failed relationship, she still has feelings for women and proceeded to recommend hospitalization as well as 12 sessions of electroshock therapy as the last form of treatment available:

Dr. Bandshahi said that it looks like that I do not want to stop these kinds of [homosexual] actions and become corrected. He said he had thought my feelings for women will end after one time of being with a girl but they have clearly not. After saying this, he asked me to leave the room and called in my parents. After sometime, he called me back to his office and said "Polina, I have prescribed you ECT". This was exactly his sentence. I did not know what ECT was. He said that his opinion is that I should be hospitalized for 20 days and remain under his care because I am at risk of committing suicide. In order for this to happen, he said he needs my father's consent. Convinced that I am schizophrenic, my father gave his permission for ECTs but disagreed with my hospitalization as he had the experience of his brother getting worse after hospitalization.

Polina subsequently received six courses of electroshock therapy, which she said resulted in extreme confusion and memory loss for about six months, and put her effectively "out of business". She added that in the years following the treatment, her speech became slurred and her eyebrows kept shaking abnormally during argument situations.

JFI & 6Rang understand that while electroshock therapy is usually recommended as a last line of intention for patients with severe mental health disorders who have not responded to other interventions such as psychotherapy and medication, Polina's doctor never provided her with effective psychotherapy to address the role of stigma and discrimination in her mental distresses and to support her in identity exploration and development without seeking predetermined outcomes. Neither did the doctor take any steps to provide Polina's parents with alternative sources of information about sexual orientation that could potentially modify their highly rejective behaviours and increase their capacity to better understand and support their daughter, thus improving her total health and well-being. When asked about the way in which her doctor discussed the associated benefits, risks and alternatives to electroshock therapy, Polina said,

> Dr. Bandshahi said that ECT is the last form of treatment available for my situation and if I do not respond to it, there is nothing else that can be done… His theory was that if I had not lived the past I had and if my father had not treated me the way he had, I may have grown up a straight girl. He said he wanted to help me solve this problem and put the past behind me. He believed that with ECT I could forget the past, my sexual orientation could perhaps get corrected and I could begin to lead a more normal life.

Farnaz, another lesbian woman, was also prescribed electroshock therapy when she was twenty-two years old in order to address the distresses believed to be associated with her same-sex sexual attractions:

> My psychiatrist diagnosed me with severe depression related to Gender Identity Disorder. She prescribed electroshock therapy instead of medication. I understand that one can take Fluoxetine or other antidepressants to be cured of her depression, but she advised no such medicine to me. I went to one shock therapy session and refused to go again, because my cognitive faculties got entirely disturbed. My memory stopped functioning correctly: I would forget everything. I would try to study, but would fail to make sense of what I was reading. It was like nothing I had ever experienced before. It felt as if part of my memory had been completely erased…I was told that the therapy is aimed at eliminating my depression and Gender Identity Disorder. My identity was considered to be pathological and my doctor presumed that it could be corrected with electroshock therapy.[1]

Farnaz reported that one of her gay friends had been also subjected to electroshock therapy for a couple of sessions "under the pretext of curing him of his sexuality."[2]

Hormone therapy is another form of reparative therapy to which lesbian, gay, and transgender individuals with gender variance have been reportedly subjected. According to Dr. Fariba Arabgol, who openly advocates the administration of hormone therapy for gender identity conversion purposes:

> Estrogen therapy is one of the methods of treating patients with Gender Identity Disorder This treatment is specifically helpful for patients who have a

---

1 Interview with Farnaz, May 2012.
2 Ibid.

disordered gender identity but do not want to receive sex reassignment surgery. Estrogen therapy causes the return of feminine characteristics in women who have a desire to be man; it also helps men with a desire to be woman to consider remaining in their original sex.[1]

Pegah, a male-to-female transsexual, told JFI & 6Rang that she was put on "testosterone" when she was twenty-one years old in order to be cured of her homosexual desires. She said the following about the pain and discomfort she experienced following this treatment:[2]

> I shared the fact that I am attracted toward members of the same sex with my neighbor who was a doctor and asked him if there was a way I could solve this problem. He referred me to an endocrinologist to help me. At that time, I had no idea that I could change my sex and become a woman... The endocrinologist I went to wrote me a prescription for testosterone. I cannot recall whether, at that point, my testosterone levels were actually low or not. In any case, he meant to boost my testosterone levels. I think it was after he gave me the first or second injection that I began to feel agitated, as if I was trembling on the inside. My groins began aching, and I began grinding my teeth. I called his secretary and asked to speak to the doctor. The secretary asked why I was calling, in response to which I said that he had prescribed an injection, and now after taking it I was feeling as I described. The doctor then took over the receiver from the secretary and asked me to pay

---

1 "goft-o goo ba doctor Fariba Arabgol darbare-ye ekhtelal-e hoviat-e jensi [Discussion with Dr. Fariba Arabgol about Gender Identity Dirsorder]" *Paygah-e Ettla'h Resani-ye Iranian: Shayad Bakhti Digar* (3 May 2008), online:
http://www.salamatiran.com/NSite/FullStory/?Id=1572&Type=2 (Retrieved March 21 2014).

2 Interview with Pegah, September 2013.

him a visit immediately. At his office, he wrote me a medical test that I had to take at a specialist ward of Namazi Hospital. After seeing the results, he said: "your body did not accept the hormone because you were mentally resistant."

In some instances, psychoactive medications, electroshock therapies and hormone therapies were recommended to lesbian, gay and transgender individuals, along with a range of behavior modification techniques, all detrimental to their psychological and emotional well-being. These included instructions to wear make-up, practice the stereotypical behaviors and mannerisms of the gender assigned at birth and date members of the opposite sex. Ali Rad identifies as a female-to-male transsexual and he received sex reassignment surgeries in his mid-twenties. He JFI & 6Rang about how behavioral modification treatments, together with strong psychoactive medications, aggravated his feelings of anxiety, confusion, depression and guilt when he was in his teenage years, leading him to attempt suicide at the age of nineteen:

> Throughout the middle school, my female classmates were inclined toward boys, and they bragged about having boyfriends. They were enjoying their bodies, because they were growing into mature women, and meanwhile I was beginning to completely hate my body. I was getting attracted to members of my own sex and developed sexual and emotional feelings for my female classmates. These made me think that there was something wrong with me and I decided to visit a psychiatrist... In my first consultation, I explained how I felt toward my classmates and how guilty this made me feel...I asked the doctor to give me some medicine to suppress my sexual desires. She laughed at me for quite a bit, and continued to address me as "miss" even though I asked her to not address me by that title...She recommended that I find a boyfriend for myself, and wear make-up. Mind

you, this was the very same doctor who is now a prominent authority on transsexuality, Dr. Maryam Rasoulian. She prescribed very strong medication under the influence of which I attempted suicide. I was in coma for three days. I had tried to do what she had asked of me, but it had not worked. I would wear make-up in front of the mirror, and upon looking at myself I would slap my face hard. I stared dating a boy on the Internet on Dr. Rasoulian's recommendation. I was supposed to meet with him in a cinema to find out how I felt in such situations. It turned out to be a very puzzling experience. In the theatre, the boy sat on my left side, and there was this very pretty, elegant woman to my right. Until the last second of the movie, all my senses were focused on this woman, and by no means was I aware of my date who sat next to me. To me, sitting next to this boy was like sitting next to a friend. All these circumstances created doubts and questions in me, forcing me to look elsewhere for explanations.[1]

These behavioral treatments sometimes go as far as pushing the lesbian, gay or transgender individual to engage in opposite-sex sexual conduct under the supervision of his or her doctor. Shahrzad is a thirty-year-old lesbian woman who did not know that same-sex sexual attractions are normal and positive variations of human sexuality until she reached the age of 18. She told JFI & 6Rang that her doctor forced her to engage in heterosexual intercourse, and concluded that she is a transsexual when she was unable to do so:

My psychiatrist told me that I should find a boy and have sex with him. He said he needed to see whether I was able to have sex with a boy or not. So I found this nicely built boy who agreed to partake in the experiment (we did not have to do it in front of the

1 Interview with Ali Rad, August 2012.

doctor, but rather according to his instructions). During a session in which this boy was also present, the doctor instructed us as to what to do. But it took about two months before this boy could even touch me. Every time we visited the doctor, he asked about the status of our sexual relationship, only to hear me say: "I can't."

After the first time we had sex, this boy visited the doctor himself to tell him how touching me felt like touching his male friends, and how impossible it was for him to sexually bond with me. He also told the doctor that I hate the odor of a man's body so much so that it makes me feel nauseated. After several months of further psychiatric therapy, my doctor finally accepted that I could not establish a proper sexual relationship with a man and therefore recommended that I pursue sex reassignment procedures. I was in the process of preparing myself for sex reassignment, and applying for a government loan to cover part of my expenses, when I was acquainted with the therapist of a lesbian friend. After lengthy discussions with this lesbian-friendly therapist, I realized that I was not attracted to men, but that did not mean that I should myself become a man. I realized that I enjoy my feminine body and sexual identity and do not actually want to assume the societal role of a man.[1]

Shahrzad's narrative demonstrates the extent to which lesbian, gay and transgender individuals are reliant on health-care workers to provide them with information, and the serious ways in which their right to free and informed consent is impaired by presentation of misleading information about the ethics, efficacy, benefits, and potential for harm of treatments

1 Interview with Shahrzad, January 2013.

that seek to reduce or eliminate same-sex sexual orientation and gender variant expressions.

It is worth recalling that informed consent is not "mere acceptance of a medical intervention." It is rather "a voluntary and sufficiently informed decision, protecting the right of the patient to be involved in medical decision-making, and assigning associated duties and obligations to health-care providers." [1] Consent is considered voluntary and informed when it is provided in the absence of coercion, undue influence or misrepresentation, and after complete disclosure of the associated benefits, risks and alternatives to a medical procedure. The findings of this report suggest that the reparative therapies to which lesbian, gay and transgender individuals in Iran are being subjected are not on the basis of informed consent as these therapies take place in a context of social stigma and prejudice, under misrepresentation, and without disclosure of the associated benefits and risks of reparative therapies, and exploration of alternative options for expression of sexual orientation.

As noted earlier in Chapter 1, "medical treatments of an intrusive and irreversible nature, when lacking a therapeutic purpose, may constitute torture or ill-treatment when enforced without the free and informed consent of the person concerned."[2] According to the Special Rapporteur on Torture, this is particularly the case when such non-consensual treatments are performed on members of marginalized groups such as lesbian, gay and transgender people because in the case of these populations, the significant power imbalance which is inherently present in the patient-doctor relationship, can be exacerbated by structural inequalities, stigma and dis-

---

1 Report of the Special Rapporteur on the right of everyone to the enjoyment of the highest attainable standard of physical and mental health, A/64/272 (10 August 2009) at para 9.

2 Report of the Special Rapporteur on torture and other cruel, inhuman or degrading treatment or punishment, Juan E. Méndez, A/HRC/22/53 (1 February 2013) at para 32.

crimination, notwithstanding claims of good intentions or medical necessity.[1]

5.3. Negligent and Substandard Non-consensual Sex Reassignment Surgeries

Medical abuses against transgender people in Iran are not limited to psychiatric settings. The findings of this report suggest that transgender people also experience serious violations of the right to health as a result of negligent and substandard sex reassignment surgeries that are carried out without proper documentation of evidence of Gender Identity Disorder and the full consideration of different possible therapeutic approaches.

In fact, the Iranian healthcare system not only fails to recognize the various expressions of gender that may not necessitate psychological, hormonal or surgical treatments, but it also engages in the administration of sex reassignment surgeries that drastically fall short of international clinical standards[2] and result in long-lasting health complications including chronic chest pain, severe back pain, unsightly scarring, loss of sexual sensation, debilitating infections, recto-vaginal and recto-urethral fistula and incontinence. The great deal of pain and suffering that is inflicted upon transgender people through these surgeries, as indicated by the cases below, is a cause for serious concern considering that transgender persons are required to undergo sex reassignment surgeries as a prerequisite for enjoying legal recognition of their preferred

---

1 Report of the Special Rapporteur on torture and other cruel, inhuman or degrading treatment or punishment, Juan E. Méndez, A/HRC/22/53 (1 February 2013) at paras. 26 and 29.

2 For a comprehensive review of these norms see World Professional Association for Transgender Health, "Standards of Care for the Health of Transsexual, Transgender and Gender Non Conforming People," Seventh Version (2012), online:
http://www.wpath.org/uploaded_files/140/files/Standards%20of%20Care,%20V7%20Full%20Book.pdf (Retrieved on 4 May 2014).

gender. The accounts of those interviewed for this report show that more often than not, individuals are rushed through sex reassignment surgeries without free and informed consent, and a clear understanding of the risks that such interventions entail.

Farzam is a female-to-male transsexual who underwent a mastectomy[1] in 2007, when he was twenty-two years old. He shared with JFI & 6Rang the growing pains and discomforts that he experienced throughout the years following his surgery:

> Unfortunately, Dr. Oskooyi turned me into a bit of a lab rat, because I was paying her a low fee for the surgery. I had no money of my own, and what I was paying her was the sum given to me by the State Welfare Organization, which was around 5 million Tomans. I had to undergo an operation on my breasts several times because the methods she used did not work.
>
> She first thought she could drain my breasts, because I had been in the habit of binding them and, as a result, they had not grown large. However, my breasts felt very stiff after the operation, and the stiffness worsened as time went by. I asked her why my breasts were swollen and getting bigger rather than smaller. She assured me that the swelling is due to the suctioning and will go away. But the swelling stayed on: one month, two months, three months, four months, and in the meantime my breasts were getting stiffer, and they had swollen all the way up to my neck. I would try to visit her for this problem, but she would not give me an appointment, because the State Welfare Organization had not paid her yet,

---

1 Bilateral mastectomy is a common surgical procedure wherein the breasts are permanently removed and the nipple complex is repositioned to give the appearance of a masculine chest.

even though she had been given a document indicating that she would get remunerated for the job in due time when the paperwork was finished. The problem persisted for a year and damaged my entire back and body ... She eventually agreed to perform another operation. This did not, however, eliminate the stiffness and fatty tissues and excess skin were left behind. So I went through a third unsuccessful surgery, and I now have to undergo an operation on my breasts for the fourth time. I have got severe scarring as a result of all these operations and my nipples have been removed altogether. So I can never go for swimming without wearing a T-shirt.

I had no one to support me throughout this process. So my doctor felt free to experiment on my body by subjecting it to operations she had never tried on anyone else before... I currently experience enormous pain in my chest and back and they wake me up in the middle of the night. In order to remove the stiffness in my chest, she removed the surrounding muscles, and in the process she damaged my muscular tissues and the cartilaginous part of my sternum. I have been to a renowned specialist in Canada and he told me that he cannot do anything to rectify the damage because my chest muscles have been removed and my ribs are damaged. Right now, I am on the Ontario Disability Support Program because of the injuries I have sustained at the hands of Dr. Oskooyi. Back in the days, I could lift a refrigerator, but now I cannot even lift a small thing. And when I do, my back hurts. Dr. Oskooyi did all of this to me because she knew I had no father or mother to support me. [1]

1 Interview with Farzam, September 2013.

Farzam's attempts to pursue legal action against his surgeon
have remained fruitless:

> Before I left Iran, I tried to file a suit against Dr.
> Oskooyi, because she had mutilated my body and my
> back was in constant pain. But all the courts I re-
> ferred to indicated that because she was a doctor, she
> could easily nullify my testimony... Even my own
> transsexual friends laughed at me for wanting to take
> Dr. Oskooyi to court. They said I could never touch
> her, not only because she was a doctor, but also be-
> cause she could bribe people and obstruct my legal
> case. So I eventually gave up.[1]

Kia, another male-to-female transsexual who underwent bilateral mastectomy in 2004 shared a similar experience:

> The doctor left behind a gauze pad in my chest and
> because of this mistake I have had to have three op-
> erations on my breast all of which have lowered my
> chances of proper healing. Moreover, I should not
> have received a formal bilateral mastectomy because
> I was small-breasted. I now realize that liposuction in
> combination with hormone therapy and exercise
> could have given me the desired presentation. The
> doctor however failed to advise me on various opera-
> tive procedures. He gave me wrong advice, operated
> on my body, and damaged it forever, just to benefit
> himself.
>
> I have prayed to God to heal my injuries but this
> might never happen. The pain of this operation will
> always stay with me because it should have never
> been performed in the first place. It was the respon-
> sibility of the doctor to provide me with accurate in-
> formation. I was only a seventeen-year-old, full of

---

1 *Ibid.*

distress and excitement. He was responsible for giving me appropriate advice and helping me with the operation. But he did not do that because he was not fair and responsible… My body would not have had to ache with every sneeze today if things were done differently back then. To this date, I cannot lift a heavy item, as that will simply exert a lot of pressure on my body.[1]

Health complications stemming from substandard sex reassignment surgeries have not been limited to back pain and chest pain. Farnaz stated that her friend, who was a female-to-male transsexual, experienced serious urinary tract infections, after the removal of his uterus, ovaries, and clitoris and was urinating blood for up to a month.[2] Mojdeh, who underwent male-to-female genital reassignment surgery, referred to stabbing pains in her lower stomach and vaginal area, and such complications as fistulas from the bladder into the vagina, stenosis of the urethra, and a vagina that was too short and small for coitus. Reflecting on her postoperative experience, she stated:

If I knew that surgery would have had such outcomes, I would have never gone through with it, or I would have at least done it in a foreign country. Dr. Mir Jalaali mutilates people. His poor quality operations have taken a serious toll on our mental and emotional health. My goal today is to try my best and prevent other members of the community from subjecting their bodies to such harmful surgeries.[3]

Unfortunately, the deep sense of dismay and dissatisfaction that Farzam, Kia, Mojdeh and Farnaz's friend express with their surgeons is not unique. JFI & 6Rang was repeatedly told

1 Interview with Kia, October 2013.
2 Interview with Farnaz, May 2013.
3 Interview with Mojdeh, July 2013.

that surgeons failed to discuss the different surgical techniques available, the limitations of each technique to achieve
the desired results, the inherent risks and possible complications of the various techniques, and the surgeons' own complication rates with each procedure with their patients. This is
while these discussions constitute the very core of the informed consent process, which is both an ethical and legal
requirement for any surgical procedure. According to the
Standards of Care, surgeons must provide patients with all of
this information "in writing, in a language in which they understand, and in graphic illustrations." [1] They must further
provide "a full range of before-and-after photographs of their
own patients, including both successful and unsuccessful outcomes."[2] The Standards of Care emphasize that patients
should receive this information in advance and be given ample time to review it carefully.[3]

It is needless to state that the current practices of surgeons in
Iran are a far cry from these requirements. In fact, surgeons
frequently misrepresent the efficacy and potential for harm of
surgeries when counseling individuals seeking surgical treatments, and approach consultations with patients as a com-
mercial interaction focused on promoting low-cost services
rather than ensuring patients' health and well-being. Pegah
who underwent male-to-female sex reassignment surgeries in
2001 said,

> In those years, Dr. Mir Jalaali's going rate for a com-
> plete sex reassignment operation was one million and
> two hundred thousand toman and I did not have that
> kind of money. I told this to my friend and she said:

---

1 World Professional Association for Transgender Health, "Standards of Care for the
Health of Transsexual, Transgender and Gender Non Conforming People," Seventh
Version (2012), pp. 56-57, online:
http://www.wpath.org/uploaded_files/140/files/Standards%20of%20Care,%20V7%20
Full%20Book.pdf (Retrieved on 4 May 2014).

2 *Ibid*, at p. 56.

3 *Ibid*, at p. 56.

"Leave it to me. Let's go to Dr. Mir Jalaali, and I will bargain with him." I remember the scene in Dr. Mir Jalaali's office very well. My friend told him: "You see, doctor, he doesn't have enough money. There are some people who can afford what you charge but this one is a laborer and he's only got so much money. So do a good thing, and earn yourself a clean paycheck in the process."

Dr. Mir Jalaali always had the attitude of a business-man toward such matters. So he accepted my friend's suggestion at a glance. He added though that he would operate on me as an outpatient so that we do not have to pay the hospital for general anesthesia. He said, "I will put you to sleep and then transform you into a woman, but a woman without a vagina." I said, "OK, but for how much?" He asked for four hundred thousand Tomans. His plan was to cut off the penis and shape the organ's external appearance into a vagina. However, he was not going to recon-struct the vulvo-vaginal complex from the inside, as that required that I be put under general anesthesia and be cut open. He performed the operation with the assistance of his daughter who was attending this kind of an operation for the very first time and an operating room technician. They put me to sleep with medication and used localized anesthesia but I could still feel a lot of pain.

After the surgery, I went to my aunt's house. Luckily she was a nurse because my surgical wounds had got infected and I had no money for their treatment. Dr. Mir Jalaali had indicated that if my infection per-sisted, I would have to check in at Mehr Hospital but this was a very expensive hospital and I could not af-ford it... I do not want to say that Dr. Mir Jalaali is a terrible doctor. At the time, he was the only person in the country who really knew how to operate on transsexual people seeking surgical treatment. But operating on people has turned it into a business for him. So he does not sometimes care about his patients the way he should.[1]

The account of Kia provides an illustrative example of how surgeons like Dr. Mir Jalaali create false or unjustified expectations of favorable results, and limit any discussion of potential harms to broad and inexact comments such as "you will never be able to function like a natural man," "you will never be a father," or "you will never have the sexual stamina of a real man":

Dr. Mir Jalaali would often tell people that they can have their operations all at once if they have concerns about their financial situation. He would also oversimplify the process and imply that he can easily remove our breasts and ovaries, insert silicone testicles and get us a cock. I used to protest and say that getting a penis was not as easy as he made it sound to be. He would, however, say "No! It grows on its own and can get as long as 12 centimeters in length." I was not stupid enough to believe him. But no, to be honest, I was actually stupid. Why should I lie? I was beginning to believe him, and the only thing that prevented me from proceeding was that at that time, I was still a university student and a member of our university's sports team and I was afraid that I would be put into trouble if my clitoris was going to grow like what he said it would. Thank God that I never went through with the procedure... In the early years, he used to say nothing to his patients about the function of the clitoris even though he knew that we did not understand his methods and their implications. He would simply say that it all depends on the patient's unique physique... In recent years, he

1 Interview with Pegah, September 2013.

has updated his methods and tells people something along the lines of "you should not think that you have will ever have a natural sexual life. Yours would be one of a "lick and suck" function only."[1]

Leila is one of the many transsexual persons who accepted Dr. Mir Jalaali's recommendation to have her orchiectomy, penectomy, vaginoplasty, clitoroplasty, labiaplasty and breast reconstruction surgery all at once. She stated in an interview with JFI & 6Rang,

> I thought this course of action could reduce my pain and save me both time and money. This was, however, a huge mistake. My upper and lower parts were deformed simultaneously and the pain was absolutely horrendous.[2]

She added that Dr. Mir Jalaali subjected her to such course of treatment without giving her any meaningful preoperative surgical consultation about post-operative care and follow-up:

> I did not have anyone to take care of me and had nowhere to go after I got dismissed from the hospital. I was thrown in the backseat of a taxi and sent away to a hostel. I was in a state of coma for three days, and during this period, the hostel staff did not even bother to check up on me and see whether I was dead or alive even though they had been told that I had been through a demanding surgery. I remember waking up from the sound of the phone, only to find myself drenched in blood. My breasts had severely swollen. I immediately went to the hospital. As soon as they saw my condition, they cancelled the operation of another patient who had been already prepared and took me into the operation room instead. I was told that if I had waited a few

1 Interview with Kia, October 2013.
2 Interview with Leila, March 2012.

more hours, infection would have reached my heart and I would have died.[1]

During this research, JFI & 6Rang learned of at least three transsexual individuals who passed away post operatively due to significant lack of post-surgical care and follow-up, and two of them were Doctor Mir Jalaali's patients.

One of the victims was a male-to-female transsexual from the city of Esfahan. Soheil who knew her through the community said:

> Apparently, she had had nobody to stay with after her operation and her friends took her to a hotel after she was dismissed from the hospital. She died of bleeding in the hotel, because she had been poorly operated on and received no proper post-surgical care. Let me add that no funeral house was willing to wash and prepare her body for burial. Even when her friends performed the ablutions, the burial grounds did not accept her body and she remained unburied. Where does justice figure in all this? It is distressing that as transsexuals we even have to worry about what happens to us after death.[2]

There is a widespread belief among transgender people in Iran that cases of injury and death resulting from medical malpractice cannot be investigated because the agreement forms they sign contain an exclusion of liability clause. JFI & 6Rang was not able to obtain a copy of these forms as they generally stay with the surgeon and the patient is not provided with a copy.

In addition to physical health problems, a number of interviewees told JFI & 6Rang that they experienced sexual harassment and violence at the hands of doctors and other

---

1 *Ibid.*

2 Interview with Soheil, July 2012.

health-care professionals. Nima, a female-to-male transsexual, said:

> I visited this male cosmetic surgeon who kept touching my breasts. He asked me to undress in the presence of his secretary... I used to wrap a bandage tightly around my chest to strap my breasts down flat and this had resulted in horrible dermatologic scarring. My breasts had turned black and blue in color and my blood vessels had got damaged... This doctor kept touching my breasts until I said: "that's enough. You've seen enough of it." He then asked me to lie down on the examination table but I refused and left instead. It was obvious what his intentions were.[1]

Soheil, another female-to-male transsexual who did his hysterectomy, bilateral mastectomy, and bilateral oophorectomy all at the same time, shared a particularly disturbing story of abuse:

> I was abused throughout the entire process of my hospitalization which lasted about 4 days. I had my surgery in a poorly resourced public hospital in the city of Karaj. I was hospitalized in the men's wing of the hospital but the hospital wrote my previous female name and the words hysterectomy and mastectomy on the identification board placed on the top of my bed. So everyone knew the kind of operation that I was about to go through.

> I was taken out of the surgery room on a stretcher, unconscious. At that point, the hospital staff and some random people in the waiting area apparently rushed toward the stretcher and began debating whether I was a man or a woman. They would look

---

1 Interview with Nima, August 2012.

at my masculine face and want to know what lay between my legs. They made dirty comments and treated me like a freak. Back then I would not allow anyone to see my body... Nevertheless, after my operation, I had become a spectacle for everybody. People took advantage of my defenseless situation and removed the covers on me to see whether I was a man or a woman. I learned about these painful details after talking to my mother. She told me that she felt like they were raping her child. She was weeping but the atmosphere was so hostile that she was afraid to come forward and proclaim me as her child.

The first night after my surgery was the worst night that I have ever experienced in life. I was left alone that night. My mother was not allowed to spend the night by my side because I was in the men's ward. Just imagine. I had been through the worst type of surgery... removing my breasts, ovaries and uterus all at once. I was in pain and bleeding. And then came the section's nurse, the one who was responsible for changing the urine bag. He forced the urinal tube inside my vagina and said in a sick voice, "don't you like this? Why did you have an operation? Wasn't it such a waste?" There I was, in pain, bleeding, and in need of peeing to somewhat relieve the pain, and this man would refuse to change the bag. I had crapped all over my bed, but the nurses would only come over to fondle me and say: "do you like this? Wasn't it a waste?" I felt like I was dying, and thought that I would never leave that room alive. Rage, pain, cruelty, abuse, I experienced them all that night. The next morning, I told the head of the ward about my experience. He asked, "They didn't rape you, did they?" I said: "no, but they did all those other things to me." He said: "go and thank God that you weren't raped." He saw that I was shocked, and added, "You asked for this operation yourself. You could have chosen not to have it." This was the answer he gave me. There was no one I could talk to about this. I had to keep it quiet. I did not want my mother to know about it as I was afraid that she might reject me too.[1]

Male-to-female transsexuals who have been hospitalized in female surgical wards have also reported stories of humiliation and verbal harassment. Nima told JFI & 6Rang:

My friends have had to register at the obstetrics ward of public hospitals. These wards are difficult places for transsexual patients undergoing sex reassignment surgery. There are usually six to seven women in a single room, all with reproductive health issues. They tend to make nasty comments and give strange looks to the transmen [transgender man] who are put in their room. Doctors and nurses address transmen by their former female name and this is a very humiliating experience. A friend of mine was really traumatized by his experience at one of these wards. He said that he is ready to beg and do anything just so that he never has to get hospitalized in such wards again.[2]

The examples of medical abuse and ill-treatment reported in this chapter likely represent a small fraction of this problem. Such abuses violate the obligations of Iran to respect and protect the right of lesbian, gay and transgender people to the highest attainable standard of health, and to protect them from treatments amounting to torture and other ill-treatment, including reparative therapies, conversion therapies, and involuntary sterilization and sex reassignment surgeries administered or enforced without free and informed consent. The

1 Interview with Soheil, July 2012.

2 Interview with Nima, August 2012.

respect component of the obligation requires Iran to not interfere with the human rights of lesbian, gay and transgender
people through policies and practices that promote or enforce
violations. The protection aspect meanwhile requires Iran to
take steps toward ensuring that third parties such as health
professionals do not treat lesbian, gay and transgender people
in a discriminatory, negligent or abusive manner, in violation
of their human rights.

6. Conclusions and Recommendations

Iran was one of the first countries in the world to allow for sex reassignment surgeries after Ayatollah Khomeini issued his 1985 *fatwa* declaring sex reassignment surgeries not only permissible but indeed obligatory "when someone is in doubt about his manhood or womanhood and strongly suspects that he has the appearance of a man but is truly a woman or that she has the appearance of a woman but is truly a man." Almost three decades later, Iran's legal gender recognition procedures have, however, become out of step with international best practices, and turned into coercive mechanisms that are more about enforcing homophobia and stereotypical norms of masculinity and femininity than about increasing respect for the rights of all people, regardless of sexual orientation and gender identity.

These procedures must be understood in the context of Iran's legal system that criminalizes same-sex sexual conduct and trans-dressing while imposing mandatory sex reassignment surgery, including sterilization, as a prerequisite not only for obtaining new identity documents reflecting one's preferred gender but also for wearing the clothes associated with members of the opposite sex. Within this legal context, individuals who do not conform to stereotypical models of femininity and masculinity are divided into two distinct yet inter-related categories: "transsexual-patients" and "homosexual-perverts." The first label is applied to those who assume gender "normalcy" through hormone therapy, sterilization and genital reassignment surgery while the second is applied to those who transgress socially constructed gender expectations without applying to become diagnosed as "certified transsexuals" undergoing sex reassignment procedures.

This dichotomous approach has placed members of the lesbian, gay and transgender community in Iran in an invidious situation where they have to "choose" some human rights at the expense of others. Enjoying all human rights is not an option available to them. They must either seek to "cure" themselves of same-sex desires and transgender expressions in order to obtain equal recognition before the law or remain marginalized and face hatred and violence, arbitrary deprivations of liberty; and widespread discrimination in areas such as employment, education and access to goods and services.

Distressed with the traumas sustained due to violence and discrimination in the family and community, and deprived of access to accurate information on matters relating to sexual orientation and gender identity, many lesbian, gay and transgender people decide to opt for the former option so as to become "legal." Aside from the coercive role played by the law, this decision is prompted by health-care professionals who misdiagnose lesbian, gay and transgender individuals with Gender Identity Disorder (GID), and prescribe to them treatments that revolve around changing sexual arousal patterns and modifying gender expressions.

Broadly speaking, these treatments fall into two models. The first one advocates reparative therapies such as shaming techniques, induced nausea, psychoactive medications, and electroshocks even though such procedures for converting individuals' sexual orientation have been internationally denounced as unscientific, harmful and a violation of human rights. The second model concedes that treatments aimed at converting one's experienced sexual orientation and gender identity are generally without success, and advocates that the body of transgender people be altered and brought into conformity with their psyche through hormone therapy and sex reassignment surgeries. Mental health professionals who follow this model are generally inclined to take social gender non-conformity, homosexual orientation, and consequences of social prejudice and stigma (such as depression, isolation, confusion and distorted self-image) as symptoms of a Gender Identity Disorder. This has rendered many lesbian, gay and transgender persons susceptible to being misdiagnosed as having a "Gender Identity Disorder," and rushed into irreversible hormone therapy and sex reassignment surgeries.

The findings of this report raise great concern that the circumstances in which such medical procedures take place do not meet the standards of free and informed consent, as prescribed by international law. Medical professionals prescribing reparative therapies and sex reassignment surgeries rarely provide their lesbian, gay and transgender clients with a meaningful opportunity to explore their same-sex desires and gender expressions, and access accurate information on issues related to sexual orientation and gender identity. In addition, surgeons performing sex reassignment surgeries misrepresent the efficacy and potential for harm of surgeries when counseling individuals seeking surgical treatments and fail to discuss with them the inherent risks and possible complications of the various techniques available, and their own complication rates with each technique. These infringements of the right to free and informed consent are cause for serious concern given reports of sex reassignment surgeries frequently resulting in serious scarring and long-lasting health complications due to negligence or lack of training on the part of surgeons in Iran.

As a party to the International Covenant on Civil and Political Rights, and the International Covenant on Economic, Social and Cultural Rights, Iran is obliged to respect and protect the right of lesbian, gay and transgender people to the highest attainable standard of health, and to ensure that they are not subjected to medical abuses amounting to torture and other ill-treatment, including reparative therapies, conversion therapies, involuntary sterilization and sex reassignment surgeries administered or enforced without free and informed consent.

The respect component of this obligation requires Iran to not interfere with the human rights of lesbian, gay and transgender people through legal gender recognition procedures enforcing mandatory sterilization and other medical requirements violative of the right to health.

The protection aspect meanwhile requires Iran to exercise due diligence to ensure that non-state actors do not violate the human rights of lesbian, gay and transgender people with impunity, including through abusive reparative therapies and negligent and substandard sex reassignment surgeries.

Justice For Iran and 6Rang: Iranian Lesbian and Transgender Network call on the Iranian authorities to:

Decriminalization of Same-Sex Sexual Conduct

- Abolish the death penalty for offences involving consensual same-sex sexual relations.

- Repeal all laws that criminalize or otherwise impose punitive sanctions on consensual same-sex sexual conduct.

- Release, immediately and unconditionally, all those who have been detained or convicted for actual or alleged consensual same-sex conduct.

Decriminalization of Gender-Variant Expressions

- Repeal all laws and regulations that impose mandatory veiling of women.

- Repeal all laws that criminalize or otherwise impose punitive sanctions on modes of clothing deemed to be in violation of Islamic dress codes.

- Repeal laws used to harass or detain individuals on grounds of their actual or perceived sexual orientation or gender identity.

Protection from Torture and Other Cruel, Inhuman and Degrading Treatments or Punishments – General

- Abolish flogging and all other corporal punishments.

- Put an end to torture and other ill-treatment in law and in practice; and ensure that torture and other ill-treatments are criminalized.

- Protect individuals from torture and other ill-treatment because of their actual or perceived sexual orientation or gender identity, whether carried out in public or in private by state or non-state actors.

- Ensure that all allegations and reports of torture and other ill-treatment based on sexual orientation or gender identity are promptly and impartially investigated by competent authorities, and perpetrators held accountable and brought to justice.

- Provide victims with effective remedy and redress, including measures of reparation, satisfaction and guarantees of non-repetition as well as restitution, compensation and rehabilitation.

- Undertake public information campaigns in order to combat prejudices that lead to perpetration of torture and other cruel, inhuman or degrading treatment on the basis of sexual orientation or gender identity.

Protection from Torture and Other Cruel, Inhuman and Degrading Treatment or Punishment – Health-Care Settings

- Enforce the prohibition of torture in all health-care institutions, both public and private.

- Safeguard free and informed consent on an equal basis for all individuals without any discrimination based on sexual orientation or gender identity.

- Remove the requirement that transgender individuals undergo sterilization and genital reassignment surgeries as a precondition for obtaining legal recognition of their gender.

- Repeal any law allowing intrusive and irreversible treatments, including involuntary sterilization, unethical experimentation, "reparative therapies" or "conversion therapies," when enforced or administered without the free and informed consent of the person concerned.

- Outlaw forced or coerced sterilization, sex reassignment surgeries and "reparative" therapies in all circumstances.

- Conduct prompt, impartial and thorough investigations into all allegations of torture and ill-treatment in health-care settings, and prosecute and take action against perpetrators where the evidence warrants it.

- Promote accountability for torture and ill-treatment in health-care settings by identifying laws, policies and practices that lead to abuse; and enable national preventive mechanisms to systematically monitor, receive complaints and initiate prosecutions.

The Highest Attainable Standard of Health

- Refrain from censoring, withholding or intentionally misrepresenting health information, including information in relation to sexual orientation and gender identity.

- Implement training for health-care professionals highlighting their obligation to treat all patients with respect, including lesbian, gay and transgender people.

- Ensure that health-care professionals meet appropriate standards of education, skill and ethical codes of conduct, when caring for lesbian, gay and transgender people.

- Ensure that medical practices, especially the provision of medical care for lesbian, gay and transgender people, do not perpetuate stereotypical notions of masculinity and femininity.

- Conduct a prompt, impartial and thorough investigation into all allegations of negligent or non-consensual sex reassignment surgeries, performed in reckless or wanton disregard of international standards.

- Abstain from imposing discriminatory practices that interfere directly or indirectly with the enjoyment by lesbian, gay and transgender people of the right to health.

- Adopt policies, practices and protocols that are respectful of the right to free and informed consent, autonomy, self-determination and human dignity, without any distinction on the basis of sexual orientation or gender identity.

- Ensure that transgender people can access the health treatments they wish on the basis of informed consent.

Recognition Before the Law

- Remove lesbian, gay and transgender identities from the classification of mental diseases and reclassify aspects relevant to the provision of health care in a non-stigmatizing health category.

- Abolish requirements to undergo psychiatric assessment and receive a diagnosis for obtaining legal gender recognition.

- Amend current policies and practices by introducing a legislative proposal that sets out a framework allowing transgender people to change their names and obtain legal recognition of their gender through an accessible and transparent procedure that does not infringe upon their other human rights.

- Ensure that state and non-state institutions and bodies put in place quick, accessible and transparent procedures aimed at providing transgender people with documents, such as diplomas or other education certificates, which reflect their gender identity.

- Ensure that all information concerning changes of legal name and gender is kept confidential, and disclosed to third parties only with the explicit consent of the persons concerned.

Equality and Non-Discrimination – General

- Repeal all laws that result in, or are likely to result in, discrimination, against people solely for their sexual orientation or gender identity.

- Provide explicit legal protection against discrimination on the grounds of sexual orientation or gender identity in all areas of life.

- Take steps to raise public awareness of sexual and gender identity diversity and the discrimination experienced by gay, lesbian and transgender people.

Equality and Non-Discrimination – Education

- Take all necessary legislative, administrative and other measures to ensure equal access to primary, secondary and higher levels of education without discrimination on the basis of sexual orientation or gender identity.

- Protect students against discrimination and violence perpetrated because of their actual or perceived sexual orientation or gender identity and hold perpetrators accountable.

- Ensure that students subjected to incidents of discrimination or violence are not marginalized or segregated, and that their best interests are identified and respected in a participatory manner.

- Introduce into education curricula modules about diversity and about the human rights of all, including lesbian, gay, bisexual and transgender people.

Freedom of Expression and Access to Information

- Repeal laws that ban positive or neutral statements about homosexuality in order to ensure freedom of expression, association and peaceful assembly regarding issues relating to sexual orientation and gender identity.

- Respect the right of all people to exercise their freedom of expression, assembly and association without discrimination on the basis of sexual orientation or gender identity.

- Introduce training for media and education professionals about diversity and about the human rights of all as including lesbian, gay, bisexual and transgender people.

Cooperation with United Nations Human Rights Mechanisms

- Ratify immediately and without any reservation the United Nations Convention Against Torture and Other Cruel, Inhuman or Degrading Treatment or Punishment and its Optional protocol; the Convention on the Elimination of All Forms of Discrimination Women and its Optional Protocol; and the optional protocols to the ICCPR and the ICESCR.

- Agree to a visit by the UN Special Rapporteur on the right to the highest attainable standard of health to make recommendations regarding best practice policies to ensure that gay, lesbian and transgender people are not subjected to human rights violations, as including torture and other ill-treatment, in health care settings.

- Give effect to the government's standing invitation for other UN special procedures to visit Iran at the earliest possible opportunity.

Terminology

Bisexuals are people whose emotional, affectionate and sexual attraction can be toward both women and men.

Dojense is a term used in Persian for referring to both intersex (physical *dojense*) and transsexual (psychological *dojense*) people. Its literal meaning is "bisexed."

Gay refers to men whose emotional, affectionate and sexual attraction is primarily toward men.

Gender refers to the socially constructed roles, behaviors, activities, and attributes that a given society considers appropriate for men and women.

Gender Expression refers to the means by which individuals express their gender identity. This may or may not include dress, make-up, speech, mannerisms and surgical or hormonal treatment.

Gender Identity is a very personal and subjective matter. It refers to each person's deeply felt internal and individual experience of gender, which may or may not correspond with the sex assigned at birth. It includes the personal sense of the body (which may involve, if freely chosen, modification of bodily appearance or function by medical, surgical or other means) and other expressions of gender, including dress, speech and mannerism.

Gender Identity Disorder or Gender Dysphoria is a discomfort characterized by a feeling of incongruity with the physical gender assigned to one at birth. Frequently misunderstood by the individual, these feelings can remain suppressed and hidden from others. Unhealthy coping mechanisms include self-abuse, addictions, relationship difficulties and suicidality.

Gender Identity Disorder may be experienced by biological males or females of any cultural, ethnic or socioeconomic background. In 2013, the American Psychiatric Association updated the term "Gender Identity Disorder" to "Gender Dysphoria" in the fifth version of the Diagnostic Manual of Mental Disorders (DSM-V). However, the former term will be used throughout this report.

Gender Marker is a gendered designator that appears on an official document such as a passport or an identity card. It may be an explicit designation such as "male" or "female" or a gendered title such like Mr. or Ms.

Gender Queer refers to gender identities other than "man" and "woman," thus falling outside of the gender binary.

Genital Reassignment Surgeries refer to operations aimed at modifying genital characteristics to accord with a person's gender identity. They include gonad removal and genital removal as well as reconstructive procedures such as orchidectomy, penectomy, genito-vaginoplasty or labiaplasty for the male-to-female individuals; or vaginectomy and genito-phalloplasty for female-to-male individuals.

Hamjensbaz is a derogatory Persian term for referring to homosexuals. Its literal meaning is same-sex "gamer" and it implies that homosexuals are people with loose morals who chase people of the same sex for sexual pleasure.

Heterosexual people are individuals whose emotional, affectionate and sexual attraction is primarily to members of the opposite sex.

Heteronormativity refers to a system of norms, attitudes and biases that assumes that people fall into distinct and complementary genders (man and woman) with natural roles in life. It asserts that heterosexuality is the normal sexual orientation, and sexual and marital relations are only fitting between a man and a woman. Consequently, a "heteronormative" view is one that involves alignment of biological sex, sexuality, gender identity, and gender roles.

Homosexual people are individuals whose emotional, affectionate and sexual attraction is primarily to members of the same sex.

Hormone Therapy or Hormone Replacement Therapy (HRT) is a form of medical treatment that transgender people may wish to take in order to develop some secondary sex characteristics of the gender with which they more closely identify. Irreversible effects testosterone on female-to-male transsexuals include deepening of voice, growth of facial and body hair, and enlargement of the clitoris while reversible effects include cessation of ovulation and menstruation and muscle development. Partially reversible effects of estrogen on male-to-female transgenders include breast tissue growth (gynaecomastia), and reversible changes include lightening of body hair, smoother skin and reduction in testicle and gonad size. Estrogen has no effect on male-to-female transgenders' voice pitch.

Intersex individuals possess genital, chromosomal or hormonal characteristics that do not correspond to the given standard for the "male" or "female" categories of the sexual or reproductive anatomy. Intersexuality may take different forms and cover a wide range of conditions.

Lesbians are women whose emotional, affectionate and sexual attraction is primarily toward women.

Sex refers to the biological classification of bodies as male or female based on a range of biological and physiological characteristics including external sex organs, internal sexual and reproductive organs, hormones, and chromosomes.

Sex Change refers to the process through which a person modifies his or her physical characteristics to be consistent with his or her gender identity. This transition may include hormone therapy, sex reassignment surgery and other medical procedures such as hysterectomy and mastectomy, and is generally conducted under medical supervision based on a set of standards developed by medical professionals. **Sex Reassignment Surgeries** refer to a range of medical treatments that a transgender person may wish to undergo. Treatments may include sex reassignment surgery including facial surgery, chest surgery, genital or gonad surgery, and can include sterilization. Not all transgender people feel a need to undergo sex reassignment surgeries.

Sexual Minorities are groups whose sexual identity, orientation or practices differ from the majority of the surrounding society. The term refers primarily to lesbian, gay, bisexual and transgender people. These four categories are often grouped together under the rubric LGBT. Some LGBT people object to using the term sexual minorities because they do not want to be considered a distinct minority but an integral part of the society. Some transsexual and transgender people meanwhile believe that it is inaccurate to classify them as a sexual minority because the phenomenon of transsexuality or transgenderism is less related to sexual orientation and practices and more related to gender, and gender-variant behavior or feelings.

Sexual Orientation refers to each person's capacity for profound emotional, affectionate and sexual attraction to, and intimate and sexual relations with, individuals of a different gender or the same gender or more than one gender.

Trans-dressing describes the act of wearing clothes mostly associated with a gender other than the gender the individual was assigned at birth.

Transgender people are individuals whose gender expression and/or gender identity differs from conventional expectations based on the physical sex they were assigned at birth. A male-to-female transgender individual is a woman who was assigned the "male" sex at birth but has a "female" gender identity; a female-to-male transgender person is a man who was assigned the "female" sex at birth but has a "male" gender identity. Not all transgender individuals identify as male or female; "transgender" is a term that includes members of third genders, as well as individuals who identify as more than one gender or no gender at all. Transgender individuals may or may not choose to undergo some, or all, possible forms of sex reassignment surgeries.

Transgender Man is an individual who was assigned the "female" sex at birth but identifies himself as a man. They are sometimes referred to as "transmen."

Transgender Woman is an individual who was assigned the "male" sex at birth but identifies herself as a woman. They are sometimes referred to as "transwomen."

Transsexual individuals have a gender expression and/or gender identity that differs from conventional expectations based on the physical sex they were assigned at birth and who wish to undergo, are in the process of undergoing or have undergone, sex reassignment surgeries. Transsexual individuals transitioning from male to female are sometimes referred to as "MtF" and transsexual individuals transitioning from Female to male as "FtM."

Bibliography

International Treaties, Conventions and Other international instruments

1. Basic Principles and Guidelines on the Right to a Remedy and Reparation for Victims of Gross Violations of International Human Rights Law and Serious Violations of International Humanitarian Law, A/Res/60/147 (21 March 2006).
2. Committee against Torture, General Comment No. 2 (CAT/C/GC/2)
3. Committee against Torture, General Comment No. 2: Implementation of Article 2 by States Parties, CAT/C/GC/2/CRP. 1/Rev.4 (23 November 2007)
4. Committee on Economic Social and Cultural Rights, General Comment No. 20, E/C.12/GV/20 (2009)
5. Committee on Economic Social and Cultural Rights, General Comment No. 14 (E/C/12/2000/4)
6. Committee on Economic, Social and Cultural Rights, General Comment No. 14: The right to the highest attainable standards of health, E/C.12/2000/4 (11 August 2000)
7. Committee on Economic, Social and Cultural Rights, General Comment No. 20 (E/C.12/GC/20), 2 July 2009
8. Committee on Economic, Social and Cultural Rights, General Comment No. 31: The Nature of the General Legal Obligation Imposed on States Parties to the Covenant, CCPR/C/21/Rev.1/Add.13, 26 May 2004
9. Committee on Economic, Social and Cultural Rights, General comment No. 3: The Nature of States Parties' Obligations, E/1991/23 (14 December 1990)
10. Committee on Economic, Social and Cultural Rights, General comment No. 9: The domestic application of the Covenant, E/C.12/1998/24 (3 December 1998)
11. Committee on Economic, Social and Cultural Rights, General comment No. 19: *The right to social security*, E/C.12/GC/19 (4 February 2008)
12. Committee on the Elimination of Discrimination against Women, General Recommendation No. 28 (CEDAW/C/GC/28)
13. Committee on the Rights of the Child general comments No. 3 (CRC/GC/2003/3)
14. Committee on the Rights of the Child, Concluding observations on New Zealand (CRC/C/NZL/CO/3-4)
15. Committee on the Rights of the Child, Concluding observations on Slovakia (CRC/C/SVK/CO/2)
16. Committee on the Rights of the Child, Concluding observations on Malaysia (CRC/C/MYS/CO/1)

17. Committee on the Rights of the Child, Concluding observations on Chile (CCPR/C/CHL/CO/5) - Committee on the Rights of the Child, Concluding observations on San Marino (CCPR/C/SMR/CO/2), Committee on the Rights of the Child's on Austria (CCPR/C/AUT/CO/4)
18. Committee on the Rights of the Child, General Comment No. 13 (CRC/C/GC/13)
19. Committee on the Rights of the Child, General Comment No. 4, CRC/GC/2003/4 (2003).
20. Concluding observations of the Committee on Economic, Social and Cultural Rights on Poland (E/C.12/POL/CO/5)
21. Concluding observations of the Human Rights Committee on El Salvador (CCPR/C/SLV/CO/6
22. Concluding observations of the Human Rights Committee on Finland (CCPR/CO/82/FIN)
23. Concluding observations of the Human Rights Committee on Greece (CCPR/CO /83/GRC)
24. Concluding observations of the Human Rights Committee on Mexico (CCPR/C/MEX/CO/5)
25. Concluding observations of the Human Rights Committee on Slovakia (CCPR/CO/78/SVK)
26. Human Rights Committee, communication no. 1361/2005 (CCPR/C/89/D/1361/2005
27. Human Rights Committee, Concluding observations on Mexico (CCPR/C/MEX/CO/5)
28. Human Rights Committee, Concluding observations on Uzbekistan (CCPR/C/UZB/CO/3)
29. Human Rights Committee, *Fedotova v. Russia*, Communication No. 1932/2010 (CCPR/C/106/D/1932/2010)
30. Human Rights Committee, General Comment No. 16: Article 17 (Right to Privacy), The Right to Respect of Privacy, Family, Home and Correspondence, and Protection of Honour and Reputation,
31. Human Rights Committee, General Comment No. 31: Nature of the General Legal Obligation Imposed on States Parties to the Covenant, CCPR/C/21/Rev.1/Add.13 (26 May 2004)
32. Human Rights Committee, General Comment No. 34: Article 19, Freedoms of opinion and expression, CCPR/C/GC/34 (12 September 2011)
33. Human Rights Committee, *Giri v. Nepalxi,* Communication No. 1863/2009 (CCPR/C/105/D/1863/2009)
34. Interim report of the Special Rapporteur on torture and other cruel, inhuman or degrading treatment or punishment, A/63/175 (28 July 2008)
35. International Convention on the Elimination of All Forms of Racial Discrimination
36. Report of the Special Rapporteur on the question of torture and other cruel, inhuman or degrading treatment or punishment, A/56/156 (3 July 2001)

37. Report of the Special Rapporteur on the right of everyone to the enjoyment of the highest attainable standard of physical and mental health, A/64/272 (10 August 2009)

38. Report of the Special Rapporteur on the right of everyone to the enjoyment of the highest attainable standard of physical and mental health, A/HRC/14/20 (27 April 2010)

39. Report of the Special Rapporteur on the right of everyone to the enjoyment of the highest attainable standard of physical and mental health, Anand Grover, A/HRC/20/15 (10 April 2012).

40. Report of the Special Rapporteur on torture and other cruel, inhuman or degrading treatment or punishment, Juan E. Méndez, A/HRC/22/53 (1 February 2013)

41. Report of the UN High Commissioner for Human Rights, *Discriminatory laws and practices and acts of violence against individuals based on their sexual orientation and gender identity*, A/HRC/19/41 (17 November 2011)

42. *Toonen v. Australia*, communication No. 488/1992 (CCPR/C/50/D/488/1992).

43. UN Committee on Economic, Social and Cultural Rights (CESCR), General Comment No. 19 (E/C.12/GC/19) (right to social security)

44. UN Committee on Economic, Social and Cultural Rights (CESCR), General Comment No. 14: *The Right to the Highest Attainable Standard of Health*, E/C.12/2000/4 (11 August 2000)

45. UN Committee on Economic, Social and Cultural Rights (CESCR), General Comment No. 15: *The Right to Water*, E/C.12/2002/11 (20 January 2003)

46. UN Committee on Economic, Social and Cultural Rights (CESCR), General Comment No. 16: *The Equal Right of Men and Women to the Enjoyment of All Economic, Social and Cultural Rights*, E/C.12/2005/4 (11 August 2005) (availability and accessibility of appropriate remedies, such as compensation, reparation, restitution, rehabilitation, guarantees of non-repetition, declarations, public apologies, educational programmes and prevention programmes)

47. UN Committee on Economic, Social and Cultural Rights (CESCR), General Comment No. 18: *The Right to Work*, E/C.12/GC/18 (6 February 2006)

48. UN Committee on Economic, Social and Cultural Rights (CESCR), General Comment No. 20: *Non-discrimination in economic, social and cultural rights*, E/C.12/GC/20 (2 July 2009)

49. UN Committee on Economic, Social and Cultural Rights (CESCR), General Comment No.12: *The Right to Adequate Food* (12 May 1999)

50. UN General Assembly, *Vienna Declaration and Programme of Action*, A/CONF.157/23 (12 July 1993).

51. United Nations General Assembly Resolution No A/RES/46/119, A/46/PV.75 (17 December 1991).

52. *Young v. Australia*, communication No. 941/2000 (CCPR/C/78/D/941/2000)

Other International Documents

1. "International consultation on homophobic bullying and harassment in educational institutions," UNESCO concept note (July 2011).
2. American Psychiatric Association, *Attempts to Change Sexual Orientation, Gender Identity, or Gender Expression: Position statement* (1999) (now replaced by a position statement under the same title, 2012), available at: http://www.apsa.org/About_APsaA/Position_Statements/Attempts_to_Change_Sexual_Orientation.aspx (Retrieved on May 3, 2014)
3. American Psychological Association Resolution (APA) on Appropriate Affirmative Responses to Sexual Orientation Distress and Change Efforts (2009), available at: http://www.apa.org/about/policy/sexual-orientation.aspx (Retrieved on May 3, 2014).
4. American Psychological Association, *Resolution on appropriate therapeutic responses to sexual orientation, American Psychologist* (1998)
5. APA Policy Statements on Lesbian, Gay, Bisexual and Transgender Concerns (2011), available at: http://www.apa.org/about/policy/booklet.pdf (Retrieved on May 3, 2014).
6. Gender Identity Disorder Sub-Workgroup of the DSM-V Task Force, "Memo Outlining Evidence for Change for Gender Identity Disorder in the DSM-5" (20130) 42 *Arch Sex Behav* 901
7. Response of the World Professional Association for Transgender Health to the Proposed DSM 5 Criteria for Gender Incongruence (by DeCuypere, G. Knudson G. & Bockting, W. airs of the WPATH consensus building process on recommendations for revision of the DSM diagnoses of Gender Identity Disorders), May 2010, available at: http://www.wpath.org/uploaded_files/140/files/WPATH%20Reaction%20to%20the%20proposed%20DSM%20-%20Final.pdf (Retrieved on 4 May 2014).
8. Therapies to Change Sexual Orientation Lack Medical Justification and Threaten Health" (PAHO/WHO, 2012), available at: http://www.paho.org/hq/index.php?option=com_content&view=article&id=6803%3A%5C%22therapies%5C%22-to-change-sexual-orientation-lack-medical-justification-and-threaten-health-&catid=740%3Anews-press-releases&Itemid=1926&lang=en (Retrieved on May 3, 2014).
9. Transgender Mental Health: Discussions of Mental Health Issues for Gender Variant and Trangender Individuals, Friends and Family with posts by NYC Psychotherapist Ami B. Kaplan, LCSW, available at: http://tgmentalhealth.com/tag/prevalence/ (retrieved 18 June 2014).
10. World Professional Association for Transgender Health, "Standards of Care for Gender Identity Disorders," Sixth Version

(2001), available at: www.wpath.org/Documents2/socv6.pdf, (Retrieved on 4 May 2014)

11. World Professional Association for Transgender Health, "Standards of Care for the Health of Transsexual, Transgender and Gender Non Conforming People," Seventh Version (2012), available at:
http://www.wpath.org/uploaded_files/140/files/Standards%20of%20Care,%20V7%20Full%20Book.pdf (Retrieved on 4 May 2014).

12. WPATH, World Professional Association for Transgender Health, Board of Directors, *WPATH De-Psychopathologisation Statement* (2010), available at:
http://tgmentalhealth.com/2010/05/26/wpath-releases-de-psychopathologisation-statement-on-gender-variance/ (Retrieved on May 3, 2014).

13. Yogyakarta Principles on the application of international human rights law in relation to sexual orientation and gender identity, available at:
http://www.yogyakartaprinciples.org/principles_en.htm (Retrieved on 15 January 2014).

Regional Conventions and Treaties and jurisprudence

1. Austrian Administrative High Court, No. 2008/17/0054, judgement of 27 February 2009.

2. European Committee of Social Rights, *International Centre for the Legal Protection of Human Rights (INTERIGHTS) v. Croatia* (Complaint No. 45/2007)

3. European Court of Human Rights, *B. v France*, no. 13343/87 (1992).

4. Federal Constitutional Court, 1 BvR 3295/07. Available at :
   www.bundesverfassungsgericht.de/entscheidungen/rs20110111_1 bvr329507.html.

5. UK Gender Recognition Act 2004 available at http://www.pfc.org.uk/GRA2004.html for more details (retrieved 26 May 2014).

National Instruments

1. Circular Number 660 Article 3, Section C (6). The text of this circular is available on the official website of the Iranian Supreme Council for Cultural Revolution, available at:
http://www.iranculture.org/fa/simpleView.aspx?provID=1722 (Retrieved on May 3, 2014).

2. Civil Code (1935), available at:
http://rc.majlis.ir/fa/law/show/92778 (Retrieved on May 3, 2014).

3. Constitution of the Islamic Republic of Iran, 24 October 1979, available at: http://www.refworld.org/docid/3ae6b56710.html (Retrieved on May 3, 2014).
4. Cyber Crime Act, Iranian Cyber Police, available at: http://www.cyberpolice.ir/page/2431 (Retrieved on May 3, 2014).
5. Islamic Penal Code of the Islamic Republic of Iran – Book V, available at: http://www.iranhrdc.org/english/human-rights-documents/iranian-codes/1000000351-islamic-penal-code-of-the-islamic-republic-of-iran-book-five.html#.U2W4GK1dVLw (Retrieved on May 3, 2014).
6. Islamic Penal Code of the Islamic Republic of Iran – Books I-II, available at: http://www.iranhrdc.org/english/human-rights-documents/iranian-codes/1000000455-english-translation-of-books-1-and-2-of-the-new-islamic-penal-code.html#.U2W3cq1dVLw (Retrieved on May 3, 2014).
7. Islamic Penal Code of the Islamic Republic of Iran (2013) – Book II, available at: http://rc.majlis.ir/fa/news/show/845002 (Retrieved on May 3, 2014).
8. Press Law can , Ministry of Culture and Islamic Guidance, available at: http://press.farhang.gov.ir/fa/rules/laws2 (Retrieved on May 3, 2014).
9. Ruhullah Khomeini, "Changing of Sex, Issues 1 and 2" in *Tahrir al-wasila*, vol. 2 (Qum: Mu'assasah-I Tanzim va Nashr-I asr-I Imam Khomeini, 2000, available at: https://www.youtube.com/watch?v=8Wh0snjDCX0 (Retrieved on 18 June 2014).
10. The Education and Research Bureau of the Islamic Republic of Iran Broadcasting "Gender Disorders (Transsexuals)" (prepared by Mohammad Ali Ganji), 22 June 2008
11. The List of Examples of Criminal Content, Iran's Cyber Police, available at: http://www.cyberpolice.ir/page/2551 (Retrieved on May 3, 2014).

Academic Sources

1. " Behnam Ohadi et al, "Brain Imaging Characteristics of the Brain in Patients with Gender Identity Disorder and Normal Individuals" (Fall 2007) 9(3) *Advancements in Cognitive Science* 20, available at: http://sid.ir/Fa/VEWSSID/J_pdf/68113863508.pdf (Retrieved on 4 May 2014).
2. Afsaneh Najmabadi, "Transing and Tanspasing Across Sex-Gender Walls in Iran" (2008) 36(3-4) Women's Studies Quarterly 23-42, available at: http://dash.harvard.edu/bitstream/handle/1/2450776/Najmabadi_Transing.pdf (Retrieved on May 3, 2014); Afsaneh Najmabadi, "Mapping Transformations of Sex, gender and Sexuality in modern Iran" (2005) 49(2) *Social Analysis* 72.

3. Afsaneh Najmabadi, Professing Selves: Transsexuality and Same-Sex Desire in Contemporary Iran (Duke University Press, 2014).

4. Dr. Alireza Zahiroddin et al, "ravan darman-i movaffaghiat amiz-i chihar mored-i ikhtelal-i hoviat-i jensi [Effective Psychotherapeutic Treatment of Four Cases of Gender Identity Disorder]" (Spring 2005) 37 *Majaley-i Elmi-i Pezeshky-i Qanuni Scientific* 37 [The Scientific Journal of the Legal Medicine Organization], available at: http://www.sid.ir/fa/VEWSSID/J_pdf/60613843707.pdf (Retrieved on 4 May 2014).

5. Dr. Hamid Reza Attar and Dr. Maryam Rasoulian, "Tashkhiz-i avvalyeh-i ikhtelal-i hoviat-i jensi [The Initial Determination of Gender Identity Disorder]" (2003) 3 *Andisheh va Raftar* 10.

6. Elizabeth M. Bucar, "Bodies at the Margins: The Case of Transsexuality in Catholic and Shia Ethics" (2010) 38(4) *Journal of Religious Ethics* 601; Paula Sanders, "Gendering the Ungendered Body: Hermaphrodites in Medieval Islamic Law" in *Women in Middle Eastern History*, eds. Beth Baron and Nikki R. Keddi (New Haven and London: Yale University Press, 1991).

7. M. Nowak, "What Practices Constitute Torture?" *Human Rights Quarterly* 28(2006), quoting from A. Boulesbaa, *The UN Convention on Torture and the Prospects for Enforcement* (Martinus Nijhoff Publishers, 1999).

8. Mål nr 1968-12, Kammarrätten i Stockholm, Avdelning 03, available
at: http://du2.pentagonvillan.se/images/stories/Kammarrttens_dom_-_121219.pdf

9. Mehdi Saberi, Saeedeh Sadat Mostafavi and Maryam Delavari, "Barresy-i moghayesehyee-i ravand-i irja'-i motaghazian-i amal-i jarrahy-i jensiat beh kommission-i pezeshki-i qanuny-i Tehran ba tavajjoh deh standardhay-i beinolmelali [A comparative review of the procedures of referral of sex change candidates to the Commission of Tehran's Legal Medicine Organization in light of International Standards] (Fall 2010) 59 *Pezeshki Qanuny* 205

10. Paula Sanders, "Gendering the Ungendered Body: Hermaphrodites in Medieval Islamic Law," in *Women in Middle Eastern History*, eds. Beth Baron and Nikki R. Keddi (New Haven and London: Yale University Press, 1991)

11. Raha Bahreini, "From Perversion to Pathology: Discourses and Practices of Gender Policing in the Islamic Republic of Iran" (2008) 5(1) *Muslim World Journal of Human Rights* Art. 2.

12. Seyed Hossein Hashemi, "Fazlollah va taghire jensiat az manzare Quran" [Allah and Sex Change from the Perspective of Quran" (2011) 65-66 *Quranic Studies*155.

13. Shadi Sadr, Majmooyeh-i Qvanin-i va Mogharrarat-i Poushesh dar Jomhouri-i Islami [The Collection of Dress Codes and Regulations in the Islamic Republic of Iran] (Nili Book: Tehran, 2009)

14. Ziba Mir-Hosseini, *Islam and Gender: The Religious Debate in Contemporary Iran* (Princeton, N.J.: Princeton University Press, 1999

Non-Governmental Organizations

1. Amnesty International in *"Crimes of hate, conspiracy of silence torture and ill-treatment based on sexual identity"* AI index ACT 40/016/2007 (2000).
2. Amnesty International, "Joint Open Letter to Iranian President Rouhani" MDE 13/058/2013 (20 December 2013), available at: http://www.amnesty.org/en/library/asset/MDE13/058/2013/en/f28e3e81-f329-48fc-8c7c-e23ea88dc750/mde130582013en.html (Retrieved 18 June 2014).
3. Human Rights Watch, "Iran: Private Homes Raided for 'Immorality'" (28 March 2008), available at: http://www.hrw.org/en/news/2008/03/27/iran-private-homes-raided-immorality (Retrieved 18 June 2014).
4. Human Rights Watch, *We are a Buried Generation: Discrimination and Violence against Sexual Minorities in Iran* (15 December, 2010), available at: http://www.hrw.org/reports/2010/12/15/we-are-buried-generation-0 (Retrieved on May 5, 2014)
5. Iran Human Rights Documentation Centre, Denied Identity: Human Rights Violations against Iran's LGBT Community (November 2013), available at: http://www.iranhrdc.org/english/publications/reports/1000000398-denied-identity-human-rights-abuses-against-irans-lgbt-community.html#.U2eFj_2H4ds (Retrieved on May 5, 2014).
6. Justice for Iran & 6Rang, "The violation of transgenders' right to the highest attainable atandards of health in the Islamic Republic of Iran" (2013) available at: http://justice4iran.org/english/j4iran-activities/english-the-violation-of-transgenders-right-to-the-highest-attainable-standard-of-health-in-the-islamic-republic-of-iran/
7. Justice for Iran, "Weapons of Mass Discrimination: The Islamic Republic Policies and the Economic, Social and Cultural Rights of citizens in Iran" (2013) available at: http://justice4iran.org/english/category/publication/submissions/page/2/

News Media

1. "270 Iranians change their sex every year. 56 percent of applicants seek to become women" (3 December 2012), available at: http://www.khabaronline.ir/detail/260988/society/health (Retrieved on May 5, 2014).
2. "Four times more boys than girls are hit by gender identity disorders" (date unknown), available at: http://www.khabaronline.ir/detail/260988/society/health.
3. "goft-o goo ba doctor Fariba Arabgol darbare-ye ekhtelal-e hoviat-e jensi [Discussion with Dr. Fariba Arabgol about Gender Identity Dirsorder]" *Paygah-e Ettla'h Resani-ye Iranian: Shayad Bakhti Digar* (3

May 2008), available at:
http://www.salamatiran.com/NSite/FullStory/?Id=1572&Type=2
(Retrieved March 21 2014).

4. "gom shodan-i faryad-i bimaran-i ikhtelal-i hoviat-i jensi dar haya-hooy-i jame'e [Gender Identity Disorder Patients' Cry Lost in the Chaos of Society] (18 August 2013), available at:
http://ghanoondaily.ir/1392/05/27/Files/PDF/13920527-221-10-10.pdf (Retrieved on 4 May 2014).

5. "negahi be vazyiat-i bimaran-i dochar-i ikhtelal-i hoviat-i jensi dar Iran [a look at the situation of Gender Identity Disorder Patients in Iran]" *Sociology Articles* (3 June 2007), available at:
http://sociology82.blogfa.com/post-83.aspx (Retrieved on May 5, 2014).

6. "saly 80 nafar dar Iran taghir-i jensiat midahand [Every year, 80 persons undergo sex change in Iran] *Alef*, 30 September 2008, available at: http://alef.ir/vdcau6ne.49neu15kk4.html?33122 (Retrieved on 4 May 2014).

7. "tedad-e afradi ke dar Iran taghir-i jensiat midahand [The number of Individuals who change their sex in Iran]," *Tabnak Professional News Site* (13 October 2008), available at:
http://www.tabnak.ir/pages/?cid=21203 (Retrieved on May 5, 2014).

8. "dalayel haram boudan hamjensgaraei dar eslam",(March 2014), available at: http://www.isna.ir/fa/news/93012508886/-دلایل-حرام- بودن-هم-جنس-گرایی-در-اسلام (retrieved on 18 June, 2014).

9. "tajrobeye ziste transsexual Irani", Iranian Sociology Association, (March 2014), available at: http://www.isa.org.ir/news/6473 (Retrieved on May 5, 2014).

10. Hossein Alizadeh, "Sociology Professor Fired in Iran for Discussing Homosexuality?" Huffington Post, 16 September 20130, available at: http://www.huffingtonpost.com/hossein-alizadeh/sociology-professor-fired-in-iran-for-discussing-homosexuality_b_3916652.html (Retrieved on May 3, 2014).

11. Iranian Lesbian & Transgender Network (6Rang), "Mass Arresr in Kermanshah on Charges of Homosexuality" (14 October 2013), available at: http://6rang.org/fa/news/a-group-of-gay-men-have-been-arrested-in-kermanshah /(Retrieved 18 June 2014).

12. Robert Tait, "A fatwa for freedom" *The Guardian* (27 July, 2005), available at:
http://www.guardian.co.uk/world/2005/jul/27/gayrights.iran.

13. Robert Tait, "Sex Change Funding undermines no gays claim" *Guardian* (26 September, 2007), available at:
http://www.guardian.co.uk/world/2007/sep/26/iran.gender (Retrieved on 4 May 2014).

14. Vanessa Barford, "Iran's Diagnosed transsexuals," BBC News (25 February 2008), available at:
http://news.bbc.co.uk/1/hi/world/middle_east/7259057.stm (Retrieved on May 4, 2014).

Documentaries

1. *Be Like Others*, DVD. Directed by Tanaz Eshaghian. Iran, Canada, U.S.: Wolfe Video, 2008, available at: https://www.youtube.com/watch?v=GZPkM2fZ_vc
2. "Unter dem Schutlz der Mullas: Transsexuelle im Ian" *Auslandsjournal ZDF Television Channel* (11 April 2012).

Witness testimonies and interviews

1. Justice for Iran & 6Rang, Interview with Ali, February 2011
2. Justice for Iran & 6Rang, Interview with Akan, February 2011
3. Justice for Iran & 6Rang, Interview with Leila, March 2012
4. Justice for Iran & 6Rang, Interview with Farnaz, April 2012
5. Justice for Iran & 6Rang, Interview with Nasrin, May 2012
6. Justice for Iran & 6Rang, Interview with Soheil, July 2012
7. Justice for Iran & 6Rang, Interview with Mayhar, July 2012
8. Justice for Iran & 6Rang, Interview with Nima, August 2012.
9. Justice for Iran & 6Rang, Interview with Ali Rad, August 2012
10. Justice for Iran & 6Rang, Interview with Mehrad, August 2012
11. Justice for Iran & 6Rang, Interview with Rayan, August 2012
12. Justice for Iran & 6Rang, Interview with Saba, August 2012
13. Justice for Iran & 6Rang, Interview with Rayan, August 2012
14. Justice for Iran & 6Rang, Interview with Elnaz, September 2012
15. Justice for Iran & 6Rang, Interview with Shahrzad, January 2013
16. Justice for Iran & 6Rang, Interview with Kaveh, January 2013
17. Justice for Iran & 6Rang, Interview with Ashkan, January 2013
18. Justice for Iran & 6Rang, Interview with Faraz, January 2013
19. Justice for Iran & 6Rang, Interview with Sohrab, January 2013
20. Justice for Iran & 6Rang, Interview with Pedram, January 2013
21. Justice for Iran & 6Rang, Interview with Hiva, January 2013
22. Justice for Iran & 6Rang, Interview with Sarah, 25 January, 2013
23. Justice for Iran & 6Rang, Interview with Sepehr, March 2013
24. Justice for Iran & 6Rang, Interview with Farnaz, May 2013
25. Justice for Iran & 6Rang, Interview with Arman, June 2013
26. Justice for Iran & 6Rang, Interview with Mojdeh, July 2013
27. Justice for Iran & 6Rang, Interview with Solmaz, July 2013
28. Justice for Iran & 6Rang, Interview with Amirali, August 2013
29. Justice for Iran & 6Rang, Interview with Pegah, September 2013
30. Justice for Iran & 6Rang, Interview with Sayeh, September 2013
31. Justice for Iran & 6Rang, Interview with Shiva September 2013
32. Justice for Iran & 6Rang, Interview with Kia, October 2013
33. Justice for Iran & 6Rang, Interview with Mohammad, October 2013
34. Justice for Iran & 6Rang, Interview with Mehran, November 2013
35. Justice for Iran & 6Rang, Interview with Fariba, March 2014